MW00803594

Say It Like Miss Austen

Austen

A Jane Austen Phrase Thesaurus

Stefan Scheuermann

"Say It Like Miss Austen: A Jane Austen Phrase Thesaurus," by Stefan Scheuermann. ISBN 978-1-62137-772-6 (Softcover).

Published 2015 by Virtualbookworm.com Publishing Inc., P.O. Box 9949, College Station, TX , 77842, US.

©2015 Stefan Scheuermann. All rights reserved. No part of this publication may be reproduced, stored in a retrieval system, or transmitted in any form or by any means, electronic, mechanical, recording or otherwise, without the prior written permission of Stefan Scheuermann.

Table of Contents

Table of Contents

Table of Contents

Preface

Jane Austen is often referred to as the Shakespeare of prose, a title she earned with some of the loveliest passages of English writing ever inked and bound. Her stories are not remarkably gripping. Her characters are not out of the ordinary. She places usual characters in usual situations. But it is her use of the English language that draws our eyes perpetually back to her work.

After being soiled by the vulgarity of current expressions, readers bathe in the rich, supple, and fragrant language of Austen's novels, cleansing the spirit and invigorating the intellect. Her syntax is elegant and highly intentional; her modifiers are meticulously witty. There is nothing clumsy or haphazard in her entire body of work. Although many of her passages would be misunderstood if uttered in conversation today, the confusion would be gilded in the gleam of sophistication. To Austen and her contemporaries, language was not simply a tool for the exchange of ideas. It was an elegant art, to be admired for its beauty, as well as its functionality.

Modern expressions reflect the painful absence of art in current language usage. Phrases are cut and chopped, whittled down to convenient texting portions, fortunate to maintain the basic and primary elements of grammatical correctness. Certainly, the lovely little elegancies of Austenian language have been amputated from the body of conversational English, deemed gaudy, impractical, and unnecessary. The pen has long held the crown of eloquence over the tongue. But an obsolete monarch wears no crown and its subjects have fallen into ungoverned chaos without their historical leaders.

In an increasingly scientific society, we seem to have forgotten that functional and ornate are not mutually exclusive; that our language, while maintaining its communicative purposes, holds also the obligation of beauty bequeathed to it by the writers of its past—writers like Jane Austen.

This book intends to provide a tool for the gradual revival of Austenian expressions. Within, you will find multiple categories of expressional needs, within which are sub-categories, allowing the user to locate a specific thought or emotion to be expressed. For each entry, there is a quotation from Jane Austen's work, which expresses the same idea, but in language that is simultaneously deliciously attractive and poignantly penetrating. This book will demonstrate that the human experience has not changed, only the way we express that experience verbally. Our house of expression has been stripped of its paintings, its wallpaper and molding, its family portraits and sconces, and has been painted flat white. This book can guide us in the re-decorating of our linguistic walls, and return to familiarity the rich decorations that make the house as lovely as it is practical.

"...I could find no language to describe them in but what was worn and hackneyed out of all sense and meaning."

Sense and Sensibility, Volume 1, Chapter 18, Marianne to Edward on describing the beauties of nature

Compliments

To sing praises

"... to gratify her own heart in the warmest eulogium..."[5]
Mansfield Park, Chapter 41, Narrator on Henry Crawford listening to Fanny speak of Mansfield

To speak "... in ... extravagant terms of praise..."[2]
Jane Austen in a letter to Cassandra, Tuesday, December 28, 1808, about Earle Harwood

She "... spoke of him in terms of the highest admiration..."[8]
Pride and Prejudice, Chapter 30, Narrator on Lady Catherine's talk of Mr. Darcy

To be "...warm in his praise..."[7]
Persuasion, Chapter 7, Narrator on Mr. Musgrove after meeting Wentworth

"... the gratifying testimony of ... approbation..."[9]
Sense and Sensibility, Volume the Second, Chapter 12, Narrator on Lady Middleton & Elinor's drawings

The compliment meant a lot to her

"... the value of such homage was inexpressibly increased to.."[7]her.
Persuasion, Chapter 23, Narrator on Wentworth and Anne's conversation

I can't give fake compliments

"... I am the wretchedest being in the world at a civil falsehood."[1]
Emma, Chapter 27, Frank to Emma on hearing Jane's new instrument

3

Beauty

You're pretty

"You must really begin to harden yourself to the idea of being worth looking at."[5]
Mansfield Park, Chapter 21, Edmund to Fanny

Isn't she beautiful?

"Is not she an angel in every gesture?"[1]
Emma, Chapter 54, Frank to Emma about Jane

"... she possesses an uncommon union of symmetry, brilliancy, and grace."[3]
Lady Susan, Chapter 6, Mrs. Vernon to Mr. De Courcy about Lady Susan

"... when, in the common cant of praise, she was called a beautiful girl, truth was less violently outraged than usually happens."[9]
Sense and Sensibility, Volume the First, Chapter 10, Narrator on Marianne

Her attractiveness

"...any effect produced on the heart of man by such loveliness and such abilities..."[3]
Lady Susan, Chapter 8, Mrs. Vernon to Lady De Courcy about Lady Susan

I never saw a more innocent looking face

"...I never saw a face less indicative of any evil disposition..."[3]
Lady Susan, Chapter 17, Mrs. Vernon to Lady De Courcy about Frederica Vernon

She hasn't aged a day

"Her face ... appeared not at all altered."[2]
Jane Austen in a letter to Cassandra, Thursday, September 1, 1796, about Louisa

She thought it was pretty

She "... had not a word to say against its becomingness..."[5]

Mansfield Park, Chapter 26, Narrator on Fanny about Mary Crawford's gift of the gold necklace

They thought she was pretty

"... the good-natured world ... extolled her beauty so highly..."[2]

Jane Austen in a letter to Cassandra, Saturday, November 17, 1798, about Mrs. Portman

"... her appearance ... had thrown them into unceasing delight."[9]

Sense and Sensibility, Volume the First, Chapter 21, Narrator on the Miss Steeles & Lady Middleton

He's charismatic

"... the good humour of his countenance is quite bewitching."[2]

Jane Austen in a letter to Cassandra, Saturday, August 24, 1805, about Daniel

They were a good-looking family

"Nature had given them no inconsiderable share of beauty..."[5]

Mansfield Park, Chapter 42, Narrator on the Price family

He was okay looking

He, "... if not quite handsome, was very near it."[6]

Northanger Abbey, Chapter 3, Narrator on Mr. Tilney

Behavior

He cheered everyone up

His "... society was of material service in dispelling the gloom..."[8]
Pride and Prejudice, Chapter 24, Narrator on Mr. Wickham

Respecting her

"... highly esteeming ... (her) ... judgment ..."[1]
Emma, Chapter 1, Narrator on Emma and Miss Taylor

To see the good in others

To be "...quicksighted to every body's merits..."[1]
Emma, Chapter 3, Narrator on Miss Bates

Well done!

"Skillful has been the hand!"[1]
Emma, Chapter 6, Mr. Elton to Emma about Emma's contributions to Harriet's improvements

He was happy to help

"His gallantry was always on the alert."[1]
Emma, Chapter 6, Narrator on Mr. Elton volunteering to frame Harriet's portrait

He'd be happy to help

"Might he be trusted with the commission, what infinite pleasure should he have in executing it!"[1]
Emma, Chapter 6, Narrator on Mr. Elton volunteering to frame Harriet's portrait

"It was impossible to say how much he should be gratified by being employed on such an errand."[1]
Emma, Chapter 6, Narrator on Mr. Elton volunteering to frame Harriet's portrait

He made a good impression

He "… left the balance of approbation much in his favor."[1]
Emma, Chapter 13, Narrator on Mr. Elton's showing his concern for Harriet

Like a gung-ho rookie

"With the fortitude of a devoted novitiate…"[1]
Emma, Chapter 20, Narrator on Jane beginning her career as a teacher

He wasn't lying

"… he had not been … making a parade of insincere professions…"[1]
Emma, Chapter 24, Narrator on Frank's interest in Highbury

He put his money where his mouth was

"It was not merely in fine words or hyperbolical compliment that he paid his duty…"[1]
Emma, Chapter 24, Narrator on Frank's treatment of Mrs. Weston

He's been so nice

"It is impossible to do justice to the hospitality of his attentions towards me…"[2]
Jane Austen in a letter to Cassandra, Tuesday, August 27, 1805, about Edward Bridges

She's polite

Her "… manners are just what they ought to be."[5]
Mansfield Park, Chapter 7, Fanny to Edmund about Mrs. Grant

She wasn't being selfish

"… she had not consulted merely her own gratification…"[6]
Northanger Abbey, Chapter 13, Narrator on Catherine refusing the Clifton scheme

She's well-behaved/traditional

She is "...strict in her notions of decorum..."[7]
Persuasion, Chapter 2, Narrator on Lady Russell

She was friendly

She "... was strongly endowed by nature with a turn for being uniformly civil and happy..."[9]
Sense and Sensibility, Volume the First, Chapter 19, Narrator on Mrs. Palmer

She's well behaved in public

"... she is all gentleness and mildness when anybody is by."[3]
The Watsons, Elizabeth to Emma about Margaret

They were kind

They "... had their share in every exertion of benevolence..."[3]
Sanditon, Chapter 10, Narrator on Mr. Parker's siblings

Nice & casual

"... with all the unceremoniousness of perfect amity."[1]
Emma, Chapter 12, Narrator on Mr. Knightley's behavior toward Emma

He didn't dilly-dally

"He always moved with the alertness of a mind which could neither be undecided nor dilatory..."[1]
Emma, Chapter 45, Narrator on Mr. Knightley leaving for London

Taking good care of them

"... preserving them ... with reverential care..."[6]
Northanger Abbey, Chapter 20, Narrator on General Tilney and the abbey windows

Accomplishments

Aren't these all your drawings?

"Is not this room rich in specimens of your landscapes and flowers!"[1]
Emma, Chapter 6, Mr. Elton to Emma encouraging her to draw Harriet's portrait

That was awesome!

"It was the rendezvous of every good quality..."[10]
Love and Friendship, Letter 3rd, Laura to Marianne about her set of accomplishments

What she did impressed me

"It gave her a very strong claim on my good-will."[5]
Mansfield Park, Chapter 16, Edmund to Fanny on Mary Crawford's defense of Fanny

Well done

It is "... much applauded as an act of virtue on your part."[2]
Jane Austen in a letter to Cassandra, Saturday, August 24, 1805, about Cassandra accompanying Harriot

She's good at the piano

"Her eloquence lies in her fingers; they were most fluently harmonious."[2]
Jane Austen in a letter to Cassandra, Saturday, August 24, 1805, about Miss Hatton

I thought it looked good

I "... received no inconsiderable pleasure from the sight."[8]
Pride and Prejudice, Chapter 6, Sir William to Mr. Darcy on seeing him dance

She toughed it out

"... she would bear up with fortitude under this misfortune."[9]
Sense and Sensibility, Volume the Second, Chapter 10, Narrator on Mrs. Dashwood's hope for Marianne

Intelligence & Education

He was complex and unpredictable

He "... was so odd a mixture of quick parts, sarcastic humour, reserve, and caprice..."[8]
Pride and Prejudice, Chapter 1, Narrator on Mr. Bennet

You've thought of everything

"I honour you your circumspection."[8]
Pride and Prejudice, Chapter 2, Mr. Bennet to Mrs. Bennet

"... you have been obviating every impediment to the present scheme..."[9]
Sense and Sensibility, Volume the Second, Chapter 3, Elinor to Mrs. Dashwood about the trip to London

Smart

"... without any deficiency of useful understanding..."[1]
Emma, Chapter 4, Narrator on Mr. Elton

She was educated

"... her ... understanding had received every advantage of discipline and culture..."[1]
Emma, Chapter 20, Narrator on Jane's education under Col. Campbell

Smart talk

"... the wit and charms which shone resplendent in the conversation..."[10]
Frederic and Elfrida, Chapter 2, Narrator on Rebecca speaking to Frederic & Elfrida

You're smart

"... I cannot refrain from expressing my raptures at the engaging qualities of your mind..."[10]
Frederic and Elfrida, Chapter 2, Frederic & Elfrida to Rebecca

Well-spoken people are respected

"Consideration and esteem as surely follow command of language as admiration waits on beauty..."[3]
Lady Susan, Chapter 16, Lady Susan to Mrs. Johnson

You're not stupid, don't even think it

"Spread no malicious slander upon your Understanding, within the Precincts of your Imagination."[2]
Jane Austen in a letter to Fanny Knight, Friday, February 21, 1817

She knew more

She "... had a very decided advantage in discussing such points."[6]
Northanger Abbey, Chapter 4, Narrator on Isabella's conversations with Catherine

He's well-spoken

"... he has ... delicacy of language enough to embody his own ideas."[5]
Mansfield Park, Chapter 30, Henry Crawford to Mary Crawford about Admiral Crawford

She was wise

Her "... knowledge of the world made her judgment very generally and deservedly looked up to..."[5]

Mansfield Park, Chapter 36, Mary Crawford to Fanny about her late aunt

She gets it

"Her sensibility seems to be opening to the perception of ..."[2] it.

Jane Austen in a letter to Anna Lefroy, Sunday, June 23, 1816, about Cassy and "great actions"

Reputation & Popularity

Popular

"... exciting ... rather more than the usual interest."[1]

Emma, Chapter 11, Narrator on the Knightleys' visit

They're awesome!

"It is not in my power to do justice to their merits..."[10]

Catherine, Catherine to Camilla about the Wynnes

She has a good reputation

"... they say that she has always been remarkable for the propriety of her behaviour..."[2]

Jane Austen in a letter to Cassandra, Monday, November 30, 1800, about Miss Wapshire

They were popular

"Their acquaintance was exceedingly sought after."[7]

Persuasion, Chapter 15, Narrator on the Elliots in Bath

They had a good reputation

"… they had lived in so respectable a manner as to engage the general good opinion of their surrounding acquaintances."[9]

Sense and Sensibility, Volume the First Chapter 1, Narrator on the Dashwood family

Patience

She's very patient

"… and her temper excellent in its power of forbearance…"[1]

Emma, Chapter 33, Mr. Knightley to Emma about Jane

He was unaffected

"He kept his countenance extremely well…"[10]

The Three Sisters, Narrator on Mr. Brudenell hearing Mary talk of her engagement

She's such a saint

"What a prodigious innate love of virtue she must have…"[2]

Jane Austen in a letter to Cassandra, Saturday, October 27, 1798, about Earle Harwood's wife

He let it roll off his shoulders

"… he listened to all their impertinence with the most forbearing courtesy."[8]

Pride and Prejudice, Chapter 23, Narrator on Sir William receiving the Bennets' protestations to Charlotte's engagement

Humility

She was humble

"... never was there a human creature who would so designedly suppress her own merit."[1]
Emma, Chapter 50, Frank in a letter to Mrs. Weston, about Jane

She "... eagerly disclaimed all extraordinary merit..."[8]
Pride and Prejudice, Chapter 24, Narrator on Jane's response to Elizabeth's compliments

Keeping himself humble

"... properly depreciating his own abilities..."[5]
Mansfield Park, Chapter 6, Narrator on Henry Crawford's offer to assist Mr. Rushworth

She was humbler

She "... could better bear a subordinate situation."[5]
Mansfield Park, Chapter 21, Narrator on Julia compared to Maria

Who can make fun of you when you are so humble

"Your humility ... must disarm reproof."[8]
Pride and Prejudice, Chapter 10, Elizabeth to Mr. Bingley

General Character

He's perfect

"I do not see how he could be mended."[2]
Jane Austen in a letter to Fanny Knight, Thursday, February 20, 1817, about Henry

She's friendly

"... her manners have all the recommendations of Ease & goodhumour & unaffectedness..."[2]
Jane Austen in a letter to Cassandra, Saturday, November 6, 1813, about Lady Honeywood

She's sweet

"Her manners are as unaffected & pleasing as ever."[2]
Jane Austen in a letter to Cassandra, Thursday, May 20, 1813, about Charlotte Craven

She's lovable

"She is quite after one's own heart..."[2]
Jane Austen in a letter to Cassandra, Saturday, October 8, 1808, about Fanny

I think she's nice

"She seems a really agreable Woman..."[2]
Jane Austen in a letter to Cassandra, Friday, December 9, 1808, about Mrs. Dundas

He's suave

"You might not see one in a hundred with *gentleman* so plainly written..."[1]
Emma, Chapter 4, Emma to Harriet about Mr. Knightley

They're nice

"...there really is nothing in the manners of either but what is highly conciliating."[1]
Emma, Chapter 33, Mrs. Elton to Emma about Mr. Suckling & his wife

"Abundance of civilities passed on all sides."[9]
Sense and Sensibility, Volume the Second, Chapter 11, Narrator on John Dashwood's visit with the Middletons

High spirited

"...with a vivacity of temper seldom subdued..."[10]
Catherine, Narrator on Edward Stanley

She is practical

"...her prudence and economy are exemplary..."[3]
Lady Susan, Chapter 14, Mr. De Courcy to Sir Reginald about Lady

Susan coming to Churchill

He was easy to get along with

He "...was of that amiable disposition which inclines to friendships..."[4]
The History of England, Author on James I

He's a better person now

"...he appeared much edified."[2]
Jane Austen in a letter to Cassandra, Monday, September 5, 1796, about Frank

Charisma

"...the warmth which might excite general notice."[5]
Mansfield Park, Chapter 12, Narrator on Henry Crawford upon his return to Mansfield Park

Her kindheartedness

"...the really good feelings by which she was almost purely governed..."[5]
Mansfield Park, Chapter 15, Narrator on Mary Crawford

You're out of my league

"You are infinitely my superior in merit..."[5]
Mansfield Park, Chapter 34, Henry Crawford to Fanny

In spite of her behavior, she wasn't a bad kid

"...with all these symptoms of profligacy ... she had neither a bad heart nor a bad temper..."[6]
Northanger Abbey, Chapter 1, Narrator on Catherine

She kept her word

"...when she promised a thing, she was so scrupulous in performing it!"[6]
Northanger Abbey, Chapter 25, Narrator on Isabella writing to Catherine

He was good-natured

"...there was such a hearty good humour, such an open, trusting liberality..."[7]
Persuasion, Chapter 5, Narrator on Admiral Croft

Naturally light-hearted

"...infinitely more fitted by nature to express good cheer and good humour than tenderness and sentiment..."[7]
Persuasion, Chapter 8, Narrator on Mrs. Musgrove

Integrity

"...the universal felicity and advantage of firmness of character..."[7]
Persuasion, Chapter 12, Narrator on Anne speculating Wentworth's thoughts

He even has a good personality

"...on conversing with him she found the solid so fully supporting the superficial..."[7]
Persuasion, Chapter 16, Narrator on Mr. Elliot & Lady Russell

She was elegant

She had "...manners as consciously right as they were invariably gentle..."[7]
Persuasion, Chapter 17, Narrator on the young Anne Elliot

He was honest

"He had no concealments with me."[7]
Persuasion, Chapter 21, Mrs. Smith on Mr. Elliot

He rolls with the punches

He has "...easiness, openness, ductility of ... temper..."[8]
Pride and Prejudice, Chapter 4, Narrator on how Mr. Bingley tolerates Mr. Darcy's manners

She was charismatic

"She had high animal spirits, and a sort of natural self-consequence..."[8]
Pride and Prejudice, Chapter 9, Narrator on Lydia

She was naturally light-hearted

She "...was not formed for ill-humour..."[8]
Pride and Prejudice, Chapter 18, Narrator on Elizabeth

She's honest

She "...is incapable of willfully deceiving any one..."[8]
Pride and Prejudice, Chapter 21, Jane to Elizabeth on Caroline Bingley

She had faith in her goodness

Of her "...rectitude and delicacy she was sure her opinion could never be shaken..."[8]
Pride and Prejudice, Chapter 23, Narrator on Elizabeth's opinion of Jane

She's approachable

"She is all affability and condescension..."[8]
Pride and Prejudice, Chapter 28, Mr. Collins to Elizabeth about Lady Catherine

He sure seemed nice

"His countenance, voice, and manner, had all established him at once in the possession of every virtue."[8]
Pride and Prejudice, Chapter 36, Narrator on Elizabeth's early impression of Mr. Wickham

Hey, it's what I do

"...I really think it my peculiar excellence..."[2]
Jane Austen in a letter to Cassandra, Saturday, November 17, 1798, about Jane's housekeeping skills

We're not so bad

"...I believe our merit in that respect is much upon a par..."[2]
Jane Austen in a letter to Martha Lloyd, Wednesday, November 12, 1800, about Jane's willingness to travel

It takes one to know one

The "...discernment of character which could so well distinguish merit."[5]
Mansfield Park, Chapter 4, Narrator on Mrs. Norris' compliment to Mrs. Rushworth

She was chill

"...her reserve was a mere calmness of manner..."[9]
Sense and Sensibility, Volume the First, Chapter 11, Narrator on Lady Middleton

I'm casual

"You know I never stand upon ceremony..."[6]
Northanger Abbey, Chapter 8, Isabella to Catherine

Hip

"...in all the profusion ... of modern taste."[6]
Northanger Abbey, Chapter 20, Narrator on the furniture in Northanger Abbey

Pretty brave

"...with a tolerably stout heart..."[6]
Northanger Abbey, Chapter 21, Narrator on Catherine's first night at Northanger Abbey

His optimistic bravery

"His sanguine temper, and fearlessness of mind..."[7]

Persuasion, Chapter 4, Narrator on the young Wentworth

 *Insults* 1

An insult

"...some illnatured aspersion..."[2]
Jane Austen in a letter to James Edward Austen, Monday, December 16, 1816, about Edward insulting Winton

A mean thought

"This is an illnatured sentiment..."[2]
Jane Austen in a letter to Frank, Saturday, September 25, 1813, about complaints of Edward Bridges' wife

Insulted

Spoken of "...most slightingly and contemptuously..."[7]
Persuasion, Chapter 1, Narrator on Mr. Elliot toward the Elliots

He insulted it

He "...made a material difference in the discredit of it."[7]
Persuasion, Chapter 15, Narrator on Colonel Wallis' remarks on Mr. Elliot's marriage

Letting the insult roll off of her shoulder

"... exerting herself vigorously to repel the ill-natured attack..."[8]
Pride and Prejudice, Chapter 45, Narrator on Elizabeth's reaction to Caroline Bingley's antagonizing

Physical Appearance

She's not that hot

"She is a disputable Beauty..."[2]
Jane Austen in a letter to Cassandra, Saturday, November 6, 1813, about Sophia

She "...can never have been reckoned tolerably pretty..."[7]
Persuasion, Chapter 5, Elizabeth on Mrs. Clay

She did not age well

"...her bloom had vanished early..."[7]
Persuasion, Chapter 1, Narrator on Anne Elliot

He did not age well

"... he was a much older man in ways than in years ..."[1]
Emma, Chapter 1, Narrator on Mr. Woodhouse.

Ugly

"... a most deplorable want of complexion."[1]
Emma, Chapter 24, Frank to Emma on his impression of Jane

She's ugly but nice

"Perhaps she is not critically handsome, but her manners are delightful."[3]
The Watsons, Tom Musgrave to Emma about Miss Osborne

It ages a man

"... it cuts up a man's youth and vigour most horribly..."[7]
Persuasion, Chapter 3, Sir Walter to Mr. Shepherd referring to the Navy

The ugliest person

"... the most deplorable-looking personage you can imagine..."[7]
Persuasion, Chapter 3, Sir Walter on Admiral Baldwin

Stress ages a man

"...there is a toil and a labour of the mind..., which seldom leaves a man's looks to the natural effect of time."[7]
Persuasion, Chapter 3, Mrs. Clay to Sir Walter

A scowl

"... a most forbidding, disagreeable countenance..."[8]
Pride and Prejudice, Chapter 3, Narrator on Mr. Darcy at the assembly

Personality makes good looks even better, but ugly is ugly

"... an agreeable manner may set off handsome features, but can never alter plain ones."[7]
Persuasion, Chapter 5, Elizabeth on Mrs. Clay

He's not quite as ugly as he used to be

"... I do not think him so very ill-looking as I did – at least, one sees many worse."[5]
Mansfield Park, Chapter 43, Mary Crawford in a letter to Fanny about Lord Stornaway

Behavior

Crudeness

"... entire want of gentility."[1]
Emma, Chapter 4, Emma to Harriet about Robert Martin

"... very distressing vulgarity of manner..."[5]
Mansfield Park, Chapter 1, Sir Thomas to his family on what to expect from Fanny

"... so far from the common decorum of a gentleman..."[9]
Sense and Sensibility, Volume the Second, Chapter 7, Narrator on Willoughby's letter to Marianne

He turned people off

"... his manner gave a disgust which turned the tide of his popularity..."[8]
Pride and Prejudice, Chapter 3, Narrator on Mr. Darcy at the assembly

She was a nosy busy-body

"... nothing was beneath this great Lady's attention, which could furnish her with an occasion of dictating to others."[8]
Pride and Prejudice, Chapter 29, Narrator on Lady Catherine's advice to Charlotte

Everyone was bothered by her social awkwardness

"The little rusticities and awkwardnesses ... had at first made grievous inroads on the tranquility of all..."[5]
Mansfield Park, Chapter 2, Narrator on Fanny's early behavior at Mansfield Park

I didn't know he'd be so vulgar

"I had imagined him, I confess, a degree or two nearer gentility."[1]
Emma, Chapter 4, Emma to Harriet about Robert Martin

Her husband's cruelty

"... the barbarous proceedings of her husband."[6]
Northanger Abbey, Chapter 23, Narrator on Catherine's imagined behavior of General Tilney to his wife

Oh, grow up!

"What is passable in youth is detestable in later age."[1]

Emma, Chapter 4, Emma to Harriet about the manners of Mr. Weston

He was standoffish

He behaved "… with reserved manners which prevented his being generally pleasing…"[1]

Emma, Chapter 11, Narrator on John Knightley

I screwed up

"… I have made an abominably stupid blunder."[3]

Sanditon, Chapter 1, Mr. Parker to Mr. Heywood about mistaking the two Willingdens

Being judgmental

Being "… unjust to the merit of another."[1]

Emma, Chapter 18, Narrator on Mr. Knightley's dislike of Frank

She doesn't give to the poor

She is "… not contributing what she ought to the stock of their scanty comforts."[1]

Emma, Chapter 19, Narrator on Emma not visiting Mrs. & Miss Bates

She's vulgar

"… there seems no limits to the licentiousness of that woman's tongue!"[1]

Emma, Chapter 33, Emma to herself about Mrs. Elton

She's rude

"Her manners are not such as can persuade me of her being prepossessed in my favour."[3]

Lady Susan, Chapter 5, Lady Susan Vernon to Mrs. Johnson about Frederica Vernon

She is a manipulative flirt

"...she has contrived by the most artful coquetry to subdue his judgment to her own purposes." [3]
Lady Susan, Chapter 11, Mrs. Vernon to Lady De Courcy about Lady Susan & Sir Reginald

The old woman is crabby

"... at her age perhaps one may be ... quite as captious."[2]
Jane Austen in a letter to Cassandra, Tuesday, December 28, 1808, about Mrs. Hookey

He's a bad influence on you

"... your manners are hurt by the contagion of his..."[5]
Mansfield Park, Chapter 30, Mary Crawford to Henry Crawford about Admiral Crawford

He was never nice to her

"She had never been able to recall anything approaching to tenderness in his former treatment of herself."[5]
Mansfield Park, Chapter 39, Narrator on Mr. Price & Fanny

She was hypocritical

"... she had been eloquent on a point in which her own conduct would ill bear examination."[7]
Persuasion, Chapter 11, Narrator on Anne's discussion with Benwick

She was mean and bossy

"...her manners were dictatorial and insolent."[8]
Pride and Prejudice, Chapter 16, Mr. Wickham to Elizabeth about Lady Catherine

It was rude

"Nothing less than the patience of a courtier could have borne without anger such treatment..."[8]

Pride and Prejudice, Chapter 23, Narrator on Sir William receiving the Bennets' protestations to Charlotte's engagement

Her rudeness

"... all the petulance and acrimony of her manner..."[8]

Pride and Prejudice, Chapter 44, Narrator on Elizabeth's response to Mr. Darcy's proposal

"...her usual inattention to the forms of general civility..."[9]

Sense and Sensibility, Volume the Second, Chapter 1, Narrator on Marianne talking to Lady Middleton

I've been crude

"I have erred against every common-place notion of decorum..."[9]

Sense and Sensibility, Volume the First, Chapter 10, Marianne sarcastically to Elinor about Willoughby's visit

He was socially awkward

"... his manners required intimacy to make them pleasing."[9]

Sense and Sensibility, Volume the First, Chapter 3, Narrator on Edward Ferrars

Being inappropriate

"... slighting too easily the forms of worldly propriety..."[9]

Sense and Sensibility, Volume the First, Chapter 10, Narrator on Elinor's opinion of Willoughby

She was mistreated

"...she had been imposed on by others in a most mortifying degree..."[1]
Emma, Chapter 47, Narrator on Emma's thoughts after being convinced of Mr. Knightley's admiration of Harriet

She's reckless

"Her systems have all the unfortunate tendency of setting propriety at nought..."[9]
Sense and Sensibility, Volume the First, Chapter 11, Elinor to Col. Brandon about Marianne

She has made a giant ass of herself and pissed off her mother

She "...exposed herself for ever to the contempt of the whole world, and the severest resentment of her injured mother."[3]
Lady Susan, Chapter 22, Lady Susan to Mrs. Johnson about Frederica Vernon

He was unfair to her

"... he has used a young lady ... abominably ill..."[9]
Sense and Sensibility, Volume the Second, Chapter 8, Mrs. Jennings to Elinor & Marianne about Willoughby

Charming cruelty

"... with the most ingratiating virulence..."[9]
Sense and Sensibility, Volume the Third, Chapter 8, Willoughby to Elinor explaining his behavior

It was a mistake

"It was a foolish, idle inclination on my side..."[9]
Sense and Sensibility, Volume the Third, Chapter 13, Edward Ferrars to Elinor about his engagement to Lucy

Vanity/Pride/Conceit & Selfishness/Greed

She's conceited

She has "...a disposition to think a little too well of herself ..."[1]
Emma, Chapter 1, Narrator's description of Emma Woodhouse

She failed to notice her own faults

Her faults were "... so unperceived, that they did not by any means rank as misfortunes with her."[1]
Emma, Chapter 1, Narrator's description of Emma Woodhouse

He's too into his own looks

"... there was an air of foppery and nonsense in..."[1] him.
Emma, Chapter 25, Narrator on Frank riding to London for a haircut

It was a backhanded compliment

It "... was not the first distinction in the scale of vanity."[1]
Emma, Chapter 38, Narrator on Emma being one of many asked by Mr. Weston for help

What arrogance!

"...all the insolence of imaginary superiority."[1]
Emma, Chapter 50, Frank in a letter to Mrs. Weston, about the Eltons' treatment of Jane

You're awfully cocky for a kid

"Upon my word ... you give your opinion very decidedly for so young a person."[8]
Pride and Prejudice, Chapter 29, Lady Catherine to Elizabeth

He's cocky

He has "... an opinion of his own consequence ... not to be damped..."[10]
Catherine, Narrator on Edward Stanley

She was self-absorbed

"Her spirits were elevated above the influence of displeasure in any one..."[10]
Catherine, Narrator on Catherine dancing with Edward Stanley

Peacocking

"...so ostentatious and artful a display..."[3]
Lady Susan, Chapter 17, Mrs. Vernon to Lady De Courcy about Lady Susan's treatment of her daughter

She's a complete flirt

Her "...intentions are of course those of absolute coquetry, or a desire of universal admiration..."[3]
Lady Susan, Chapter 8, Mrs. Vernon to Lady De Courcy about Lady Susan

He thinks he's hot stuff

He has "...a spirit... resulting from a fancied sense of superior integrity, which is peculiarly insolent!"[3]
Lady Susan, Chapter 25, Lady Susan to Mrs. Johnson about Mr. De Courcy

Selfishly

"... not out of their good Sense of Benevolence."[2]
Jane Austen in a letter to Cassandra, Friday, October 7, 1808, about the Duer's concern with the Webbes' fire

He took forever to get ready

He "... was such an eternity finding out a thing fit to be got into..."[6]
Northanger Abbey, Chapter 9, John Thorpe to Catherine about the coachmaker

She obviously thought she was better than him

"...her deportment showed rather conscious superiority than any solicitude to oblige him..."[5]
Mansfield Park, Chapter 6, Narrator on Maria's behavior toward Mr. Rushworth

She had no boring stuff to brag about

She "... had no ... information to give, no ... triumphs to press on the unwilling and unbelieving ear of her friend..."[6]
Northanger Abbey, Chapter 4, Narrator on Mrs. Allen's first conversation with Mrs. Thorpe

She listened to him brag

"... she bore with the effusions of his endless conceit..."[6]
Northanger Abbey, Chapter 9, Narrator on Catherine listening to John Thorpe

She's selfish

She is "... regardless of every thing but her own gratification."[6]
Northanger Abbey, Chapter 13, Narrator on Isabella

He was so selfish

"His own enjoyment, or his own ease, was, in every particular, his ruling principle."[9]
Sense and Sensibility, Volume the Third, Chapter 11, Elinor to Marianne about Willoughby

"... with how little attention to the comfort of other people she could act when occasion required it."[9]
Sense and Sensibility, Volume the First, Chapter 1, Narrator on Mrs. John Dashwood

What a cocky idiot

"He is the greatest coxcomb I ever saw, and amazingly disagreeable."[6]
Northanger Abbey, Chapter 27, Isabella in a letter to Catherine about Captain Tilney

He was vain

He "...was the constant object of his warmest respect and devotion."[7]
Persuasion, Chapter 1, Narrator on Sir Walter Elliot

He liked being the center of attention

"...he had everything to elevate him, which general attention and deference... could do."[7]
Persuasion, Chapter 8, Narrator on Wentworth with the Musgroves

All of that attention went to his head

"If he were a little spoilt by such universal, such eager admiration, who could wonder?"[7]
Persuasion, Chapter 8, Narrator on Wentworth with the Musgroves

Fake, selfish behavior makes me sick

"The maneuvers of selfishness and duplicity must ever be revolting..."[7]
Persuasion, Chapter 21, Anne on Mr. Elliot

A greedy, fake, and self-serving man

"... a disingenuous, artificial, worldly man, who has had never any better principle to guide him than selfishness."[7]
Persuasion, Chapter 21, Anne to Mrs. Smith on Mr. Elliot

She thought they were stuck up

She "... saw superciliousness in their treatment of every body..."[8]
Pride and Prejudice, Chapter 6, Narrator on Elizabeth's view of Caroline Bingley and Mrs. Hurst

He is judgmental

"He has a very satirical eye..."[8]
Pride and Prejudice, Chapter 6, Elizabeth to Charlotte on Mr. Darcy

She was a cocky know-it-all

She had "... a pedantic air and conceited manner..."[8]
Pride and Prejudice, Chapter 6, Narrator on Mary

He gave a snooty look

"A deeper shade of hauteur overspread his features..."[8]
Pride and Prejudice, Chapter 18, Narrator on Mr. Darcy's reaction to Elizabeth bringing up Mr. Wickham

Boasting

"... points of self-congratulation..."[8]
Pride and Prejudice, Chapter 18, Narrator on Mrs. Bennet's conversation with Lady Lucas

"... this little panegyric on her own disposition..."[3]
Sanditon, Chapter 9, Narrator on Diana Parker talking about her sense of duty

Absorbed with her own problems

"... in such affliction as rendered her careless to surrounding objects..."[9]
Sense and Sensibility, Volume the First, Chapter 3, Narrator on Mrs. Dashwood

Greed

"... those false ideas of the necessity of riches..."[9]
Sense and Sensibility, Volume the Third, Chapter 8, Willoughby to Elinor, explaining his decisions

Her ego gets her in trouble

"Vanity working on a weak head produces every sort of mischief."[1]

Emma, Chapter 8, Mr. Knightley to Emma about Harriet

He's ungrateful

He "... did not return your kindness with any cordiality."[9]

Sense and Sensibility, Volume the First, Chapter 15, Elinor to Mrs. Dashwood about Willoughby

Insults 2

Stupidity/Ignorance & Foolishness

She was surrounded by idiots

"...she was now in great danger of suffering from intellectual solitude."[1]

Emma, Chapter 1, Narrator on Emma without Miss Taylor

He was too stupid for her

"He could not meet her in conversation, rational or playful."[1]

Emma, Chapter 1, Narrator on Mr. Woodhouse

She was too stupid to stick up for herself

"...she had no intellectual superiority to make atonement to herself, or frighten those who might hate her into outward respect."[1]

Emma, Chapter 3, Narrator on Miss Bates

She's not smart

"...strength of understanding must not be expected."[1]

Emma, Chapter 4, Narrator on Harriet Smith

"... her powers had received no aid from education..."[9]

Sense and Sensibility, Volume the First, Chapter 22, Narrator on Lucy Steele

"… her deficiency of all mental improvement, her want of information in the most common particulars, could not be concealed…"[9]
Sense and Sensibility, Volume the First, Chapter 22, Narrator on Lucy Steele

Her "… neglect of abilities which education might have rendered so respectable…"[9]
Sense and Sensibility, Volume the First, Chapter 22, Narrator on Lucy Steele

She was a little dense

"She was not a woman of strong understanding or any quickness…"[1]
Emma, Chapter 11, Narrator on Isabella

He was simple

"…his talents could not have recommended him at any time."[1]
Emma, Chapter 1, Narrator on Mr. Woodhouse

She got the wrong idea

She "…was quite mistaken in that surmise."[1]
Emma, Chapter 30, Narrator on Mrs. Weston's idea of Mr. Knightley & Jane

I've been an idiot

"…with common sense … I am afraid I have had little to do."[1]
Emma, Chapter 47, Emma to herself about her matchmaking with Harriet

Her rambling

"…all the feebleness and tautology of the narration…"[1]
Emma, Chapter 47, Narrator on Harriet's description of her relationship with Mr. Knightley

She was scatter-brained

"…she could scarcely fix herself to any employment."[10]
Catherine, Narrator on Catherine looking forward to the Stanleys

"She could not command her attention as she wished."[5]
Mansfield Park, Chapter 43, Narrator on Fanny after receiving Mary Crawford's letter

I would be an idiot if I …

"…low must sink my pretensions to common sense if I…"[3]
Lady Susan, Chapter 14, Mr. De Courcy to Sir Reginald in denying his designs on Lady Susan

I jumped to the wrong conclusion

"… I have courted prepossession and ignorance…"[8]
Pride and Prejudice, Chapter 36, Elizabeth to herself after considering Mr. Darcy's letter

It was just a bunch of idiot talk

"There was a monstrous deal of stupid quizzing, and common-place nonsense talked, but scarcely any Wit…"[2]
Jane Austen in a letter to Cassandra, Sunday, April 21, 1805, about a morning part with the Cookes

What a moron

"What a picture of intellectual poverty!"[6]
Northanger Abbey, Chapter 10, Mr. Tilney to Catherine about having only Mrs. Allen for company

How can she be "… so provokingly ill-judging?"[2]
Jane Austen in a letter to Cassandra, Thursday, September 23, 1813, about Mrs. J. Austen

I'm not quick with a witty comeback

I "… may blunder on the borders of a repartee for half-an-hour together without striking it out."[5]

Mansfield Park, Chapter 9, Edmund to Mary Crawford on his frankness

Helping an idiot

"… your indefatigable patience … in trying to give him a brain which nature had denied – to mix up an understanding for him out of the superfluity of your own!"[5]

Mansfield Park, Chapter 23, Henry Crawford to Fanny about her assistance to Mr. Rushworth during play rehearsals

She had no perspective

She "… had a little disordered … powers of comparing and judging."[5]

Mansfield Park, Chapter 37, Narrator on Fanny having grown up at Mansfield

Not a big reader

"… trained up to think the alphabet her greatest enemy…"[5]

Mansfield Park, Chapter 39, Narrator on Betsy

She wasn't real sharp

"… not less unpropitious for heroism seemed her mind."[6]

Northanger Abbey, Chapter 1, Narrator on Catherine

Dim-witted

With "… vacancy of mind and incapacity for thinking…"[6]

Northanger Abbey, Chapter 9, Narrator on Mrs. Allen

She was naïve

She was "… undisturbed by presentiments … of any evil at all…"[6]

Northanger Abbey, Chapter 16, Narrator on Catherine after meeting Captain Tilney

Her crazy notions

"The liberty which her imagination had dared to take…"[6]

Northanger Abbey, Chapter 25, Narrator on Catherine's surmises of Mrs. Tilney's fate

Ignorance is bliss

To be "… indulged in the sweets of incomprehensibility…"[6]

Northanger Abbey, Chapter 29, Narrator on Sarah Morland

To be "…spared the vexation of knowing…"[3]

Lady Susan, Chapter 40, Lady De Courcy to Mrs. Vernon about Sir Reginald going to London

Their absent-mindedness

"… the general air of oblivion among them…"[7]

Persuasion, Chapter 4, Narrator on Sir Walter, Elizabeth, and Lady Russell

Ignorant and crude

"…not much educated, and not at all elegant."[7]

Persuasion, Chapter 5, Narrator on Mr. & Mrs. Musgrove

He wasted his time in ignorance

"…his time was otherwise trifled away, without benefit from books or anything else."[7]

Persuasion, Chapter 6, Narrator on Charles Musgrove

She just didn't get it

"…it was a subject on which…" she "…was beyond the reach of reason…"[8]
Pride and Prejudice, Chapter 13, Narrator on Mrs. Bennet's failure to understand the entailment of Longbourn

I don't get it

"There is something in this which my comprehension does not reach."[5]
Mansfield Park, Chapter 32, Sir Thomas to Fanny about her refusal of Henry Crawford's proposal

He was born dumb and remained that way

He "…was not a sensible man, and the deficiency of nature had been little assisted by education or society…"[8]
Pride and Prejudice, Chapter 15, Narrator on Mr. Collins

This is above your head

"…I have the highest opinion in the world of your excellent judgment in all matters within the scope of your understanding…"[8]
Pride and Prejudice, Chapter 18, Mr. Collins to Elizabeth on her objection to his introducing himself to Mr. Darcy

The insult went over her head

It was "…a reproach, however, so entirely lost on its object…"[9]
Sense and Sensibility, Volume the Second, Chapter 9, Narrator on Mrs. Jennings after delivering a letter to Marianne

What a dumb group of people

"Their table was superlatively stupid."[8]
Pride and Prejudice, Chapter 29, Narrator on the table of cassino players

She was weak and naïve

"...neither her virtue nor her understanding would preserve her from falling as easy prey."[8]
Pride and Prejudice, Chapter 46, Narrator on Lydia in Brighton

She was young and inexperienced

"The vicissitudes of the human mind had not yet been exhausted by her."[5]
Mansfield Park, Chapter 37, Narrator on Fanny having not hardened herself against Edmund marrying Mary Crawford

She hated stupid, fake people

"...she could have no lasting satisfaction in the company of a person who joined insincerity with ignorance..."[9]
Sense and Sensibility, Volume the First, Chapter 22, Narrator on Elinor with Lucy Steele

His points were stupid

"...she did not think he deserved the compliment of rational opposition."[9]
Sense and Sensibility, Volume the Second, Chapter 14, Narrator on Elinor listening to Robert Ferrars

She was blissfully ignorant

"...her simpler mind ... saved her from such mortification..."[3]
The Watsons, Narrator on Elizabeth and the inferiority of their living compared to the Osbornes

She's nice but dumb

She "...is goodhumour itself, & does not seem much besides."[2]
Jane Austen in a letter to Cassandra, Thursday, April 18, 1811, about Miss Beaty

She was finally away from those idiots

She "... was at peace from the dreadful mortifications of an unequal society..."[3]

The Watsons, Narrator on Emma escaping her siblings to tend to her father

Foolish

"With a perversity of judgment..."[3]

Sanditon, Chapter 8, Narrator on Sir Edward's tastes in literature

I have been rash

"...I have been acting with my usual foolish impetuosity."[3]

Lady Susan, Chapter 24, Mrs. Vernon to Lady De Courcy quoting Charles Vernon

Where did you get that ridiculous idea?

"...from whence arose so astonishing a misconception..."[3]

Lady Susan, Chapter 24, Mrs. Vernon to Lady De Courcy about Frederica & Sir James

She was confused

"...she came to me ... in great perplexity."[2]

Jane Austen in a letter to Cassandra, Tuesday, August 27, 1805, about Louisa Hatton & a letter from Cpt. Woodford

I don't like shallow, lewd pop-literature

"You will never hear me advocating those puerile emanations which detail nothing but discordant principles incapable of amalgamation, or those vapid tissues of ordinary occurrences from which no useful deductions can be drawn."[3]

Sanditon, Chapter 8, Sir Edward to Charlotte about his tastes in books

A mediocre private school

"...where a reasonable quantity of accomplishments were sold at a reasonable price..."[1]

Emma, Chapter 3, Narrator on Mrs. Goddard's school

She was gullible

"... she entertained no notion of their general mischievousness..."[6]

Northanger Abbey, Chapter 2, Narrator on Mrs. Morland naivety concerning young men

He ignored boring domestic duties

He "... had become indisposed for any of the more homely pursuits ..."[1]

Emma, Chapter 2, Narrator on Mr. Weston

Laziness

"Indolence and love of ease; a want of all laudable ambition..."[5]

Mansfield Park, Chapter 11, Mary Crawford to Edmund in the description of clergymen

"... all recreation and indulgences, without the wholesome alloy of labour..."[5]

Mansfield Park, Chapter 24, Henry Crawford to Mary Crawford on his intention to court Fanny

She was useless

She was "... totally indisposed for employment..."[8]

Pride and Prejudice, Chapter 35, Narrator on Elizabeth's condition after Mr. Darcy's proposal

He wasted his time away

"... his life was a life of idleness and dissipation."[8]
Pride and Prejudice, Chapter 35, Mr. Darcy in a letter to Elizabeth, about Mr. Wickham

She was lazy

"Her disposition was naturally easy and indolent..."[5]
Mansfield Park, Chapter 39, Narrator on Mrs. Price

She had "...a decided taste for... sedentary pursuits."[7]
Persuasion, Chapter 11, Narrator on the mourning Captain Benwick

"She has been allowed to dispose of her time in the most idle and frivolous manner..."[8]
Pride and Prejudice, Chapter 47, Elizabeth to Mrs. Gardiner about Lydia

You're lazy

You "... do not altogether seem particularly friendly to very severe, very intense application..."[6]
Northanger Abbey, Chapter 14, Mr. Tilney to Catherine

You have "... a decided taste for... sedentary pursuits."[7]
Persuasion, Chapter 11, Narrator on the mourning Captain Benwick

You are "... little disposed for supernumerary exertion..."[3]
Sanditon, Chapter 11, Narrator on Arthur Parker

She is a trophy wife

She is "All idle refinement!"[7]
Persuasion, Chapter 8, Mrs. Croft refuting Wentworth

Dishonesty

Dishonesty

"... an affectation of candor..."[1]

Emma, Chapter 20, Narrator on the praise of Emma's piano playing

Being a hypochondriac

Having "... all the fancifulness and all the selfishness of imaginary complaints."[1]

Emma, Chapter 45, Narrator on Mrs. Churchill

She is a good liar

She "...possesses a degree of captivating deceit."[3]

Lady Susan, Chapter 4, Mr. De Courcy to Mrs. Vernon about Lady Susan

I hate that fake witch

"I am, indeed, provoked at the artifice of this unprincipled woman"[3]

Lady Susan, Chapter 8, Mrs. Vernon to Lady De Courcy about Lady Susan

A lie

"...a scandalous invention..."[3]

Lady Susan, Chapter 11, Mrs. Vernon to Lady De Courcy about Sir Reginald discounting rumors

"...a most scandalous falsehood."[8]

Pride and Prejudice, Chapter 23, Narrator on Mr. Bingley's continued absence from Netherfield

They told mean, fat lies about her

"...how greatly they have traduced her."[3]

Lady Susan, Chapter 14, Mr. De Courcy to Sir Reginald about Charles Smith's account of Lady Susan

All of the lies you told me and I believed

"…all the accounts of your misconduct… which you, by the exertion of your perverted abilities, had made me resolved to disallow…"[3]
Lady Susan, Chapter 36, Mr. De Courcy to Lady Susan

Don't lie about it

"…do not decoy anybody … by such a lure…"[2]
Jane Austen in a letter to Cassandra, Tuesday, December 28, 1808, about their Black Butter being gone

I hate myself for believing you as much as I hate your lies

"My understanding… teaches no less to abhor the artifices which had subdued me than to despise myself for the weakness on which their strength was founded."[3]
Lady Susan, Chapter 36, Mr. De Courcy to Lady Susan

What arrogant lies

"… how many idle assertions and impudent falsehoods the excess of vanity will lead."[6]
Northanger Abbey, Chapter 9, Narrator on John Thorpe's speech to Catherine

She didn't believe her lies

"Such strains of shallow artifice could not impose even upon…"[6] her.
Northanger Abbey, Chapter 27, Narrator on Isabella's letter to Catherine

She listened to their lies

"She heard it all under embellishment."[7]
Persuasion, Chapter 15, Narrator on Anne listening to the Elliots

I hate sneakiness

"There is always something offensive in the details of cunning."[7]
Persuasion, Chapter 21, Anne on Mr. Elliot

"Whatever bears affinity to cunning is despicable."[8]
Pride and Prejudice, Chapter 8, Mr. Darcy to Caroline Bingley

"But disguise of every sort is my abhorrence."[8]
Pride and Prejudice, Chapter 34, Mr. Darcy to Elizabeth on his honesty to her

One of them had to be lying

"... there was gross duplicity on one side or the other..."[8]
Pride and Prejudice, Chapter 36, Narrator on the discrepancies between Mr. Darcy's & Mr. Wickham's accounts

Liars are everywhere
"Affectation of candour is common enough; - one meets it every where."[8]
Pride and Prejudice, Chapter 4, Elizabeth to Jane

Reputation

He had a bad reputation

"... he was not held there in much estimation..."[8]
Pride and Prejudice, Chapter 44, Narrator on Mr. Wickham's reputation in Derbyshire

To be hated

To "... be consigned to unrelenting contempt."[3]
Lady Susan, Chapter 4, Mr. De Courcy to Mrs. Vernon about Frederica Vernon

They're unpopular

"It is the fashion to think them both very detestable..."[2]
Jane Austen in a letter to Cassandra, Thursday, May 21, 1801, about Mrs. & Miss Holder

She's a useless bore

She is "... unequal to anything and unwelcome to everybody."[2]
Jane Austen in a letter to Cassandra, Sunday, April 21, 1805, about Mrs. Stent

General Character

To be less tolerant

To possess "... less pliancy of temper..."[8]
Pride and Prejudice, Chapter 4, Narrator comparing Elizabeth to Jane

He's too wimpy for you

He has "...a more yielding, complying, mild disposition than would suit your notions of man's perfection."[1]
Emma, Chapter 18, Emma to Mr. Knightley on Frank Churchill

She should mind her own damn business

"She meant to be impertinently curious..."[1]
Emma, Chapter 27, Emma to Harriet on Anne Cox's questions about the Martins

He's fickle

"...I do not altogether build upon his steadiness or constancy."[1]
Emma, Chapter 31, Emma to herself about her feelings for Frank

"...exposing one to the censure of the world for caprice and instability..."[8]
Pride and Prejudice, Chapter 34, Elizabeth to Mr. Darcy on his interference with Jane & Mr. Bingley

She's rigid

She "...had a reserved air, and a great deal of formal civility..."[3]
The Watsons, Narrator on Emma's first impression of Mrs. Edwards

She "...is a professed enemy to everything which is not directed by Decorum and Formality..."[4]
Lesley Castle, Charlotte to Margaret on Mrs. Diana

She was moody

"She was a woman of ... uncertain temper."[8]
Pride and Prejudice, Chapter 1, Narrator on Mrs. Bennet

She's a drunk

She has many rare and charming qualities; but sobriety is not one of them."[10]
Jack and Alice, Chapter 6, Lady Williams to Lucy about Alice

He was a lazy drunk

He had an "... unfortunate propensity to liquor, which so completely deprived him of the use of those faculties nature had endowed him with, that he never did anything worth mentioning."[10]
Jack and Alice, Chapter 7, Narrator on Jack

Gullible

"... endowed with a susceptible heart..."[10]
Love and Friendship, Letter 12th, Laura to Marianne about Janetta

Scum

"Base miscreant..."[10]
Love and Friendship, Letter 13th, Laura to Marianne quoting Laura Macdonald

"... proclaimed ... deep in hardened villainy."[9]
Sense and Sensibility, Volume the Second, Chapter 7, Narrator on Willoughby after the letter to Marianne

Ordinary

"...too common to excite surprise..."[3]
Lady Susan, Chapter 30, Lady Susan Vernon to Mr. De Courcy about his expectation to marry rich

He was meaner

He "... had no active kindness in comparison..."[5]
Mansfield Park, Chapter 7, Narrator comparing Edmund to Henry Crawford

Real mean

"Oh, barbarously insolent!"[9]
Sense and Sensibility, Volume the Second, Chapter 7, Marianne about Willoughby's letter

She is crass and perverted

"Hers are faults of principle ... of blunted delicacy and a corrupted, vitiated mind."[5]
Mansfield Park, Chapter 47, Edmund to Fanny on Mary Crawford

She's plain

"... I must confess there is something amazingly insipid about her."[6]
Northanger Abbey, Chapter 6, Isabella to Catherine about Miss Andrews

She got bored of him

"...the extreme weariness of his company, ... which continued unceasingly to increase ... induced her ... to distrust his powers of giving universal pleasure."[6]
Northanger Abbey, Chapter 9, Narrator on Catherine listening to John Thorpe

He was cruder

"His tastes and manners were beyond a doubt decidedly inferior..."[6]
Northanger Abbey, Chapter 16, Narrator on Captain Tilney

A loose cannon

"...a character of dangerous impetuosity..."[7]
Persuasion, Chapter 24, Narrator on Lady Russell's misjudgment of Wentworth

'Dis-ing' him

"... being unjust to his merit..."[9]
Sense and Sensibility, Volume the First, Chapter 3, Narrator on Mrs. Dashwood & John Dashwood

An old dinosaur

"... too old-fashioned to approve every modern extravagance, however sanctioned..."[3]
The Watsons, Narrator on Mrs. Edwards' acknowledgement of her own tastes

She must hate them

"How can she find any appellation for them, deep enough in familiar vulgarity?"[1]
Emma, Chapter 33, Emma to Mr. Knightley about Mrs. Elton & the Coles

I thought he was cool. It was hard to find out otherwise

"I have a real regard for him, and was beyond expression mortified to find it, as I thought, so ill bestowed."[3]
Lady Susan, Chapter 24, Mrs. Vernon to Lady De Courcy about Mr. De Courcy

She's kind of wild

She "...has had plenty of the miscellaneous, unsettled sort of happiness which seems to suit her best."[2]
Jane Austen in a letter to Cassandra, Thursday, June 6, 1811, about Anna

He seeks pleasure

He "...must have his palate consulted in everything..."[5]
Mansfield Park, Chapter 11, Mary Crawford to Edmund, about Dr. Grant

They were Christian in name only

"They had been instructed theoretically in their religion, but never required to bring it into daily practice."[5]
Mansfield Park, Chapter 48, Narrator on Sir Thomas' regrets about Maria & Julia

Way too serious and timid

"...a most untoward gravity of deportment..."[5]
Mansfield Park, Chapter 2, Narrator on Fanny's in her first encounter with Sir Thomas

Rashness

"...that eagerness of mind ... which must generally have led to imprudence."[9]
Sense and Sensibility, Volume the First, Chapter 1, Narrator on Mrs. Dashwood

They were both reserved

"...they sympathized with each other in an insipid propriety of demeanor..."[9]
Sense and Sensibility, Volume the Second, Chapter 12, Narrator on Mrs. John Dashwood & Lady Middleton

She lived in La-La Land

Her "... active fancy ... fashioned every thing delightful to her as it chose."[9]
Sense and Sensibility, Volume the Third, Chapter 9, Narrator on Mrs. Dashwood's thoughts on Col. Brandon's attachment to Marianne

I hate fickle people

"Of all things in the world inconstancy is my aversion."[6]
Northanger Abbey, Chapter 16, Isabella to Catherine on Mr. Tilney's conduct at dinner

Moods & Feelings

She felt better

"...her spirits began to revive..."[9]

Sense and Sensibility, Volume the First, Chapter 3, Narrator on Mrs. Dashwood

She was emotional

"...her sorrows, her joys, could have no moderation."[9]

Sense and Sensibility, Volume the First, Chapter 1, Narrator on Marianne

He didn't try to cheer her up

"He did not disturb the wretchedness of her mind by ill-timed conversation."[9]

Sense and Sensibility, Volume the First, Chapter 3, Narrator on Edward Ferrars & Mrs. Dashwood

They can cheer up

"... they might procure a tolerable composure of mind..."[9]

Sense and Sensibility, Volume the First, Chapter 13, Narrator on the Whitwell party's disappointment

A really bad mood

"This violent oppression of spirits..."[9]

Sense and Sensibility, Volume the First, Chapter 15, Narrator on Marianne after Willoughby left

Hey, it's not all that bad

"Come, come; this is all an effusion of immediate want of spirits..."[9]

Sense and Sensibility, Volume the First, Chapter 19, Mrs. Dashwood to Edward Ferrars

She was hysterical

Her "... consternation was excessive..."[9]

Sense and Sensibility, Volume the First, Chapter 21, Narrator on Lady Middleton when Anna-maria was scratched

In a bad mood

"... particularly ill-disposed ... to be pleased..."[9]

Sense and Sensibility, Volume the First, Chapter 22, Narrator on Marianne with the Miss Steeles

She had her head in the clouds

"... her mind was ... abstracted from every thing actually before them..."[9]

Sense and Sensibility, Volume the Second, Chapter 4, Narrator on Marianne in the London shops

He didn't make her feel better

She "... derived no comfortable feelings from this conversation to lessen the uneasiness of her mind..."[9]

Sense and Sensibility, Volume the Second, Chapter 5, Narrator on Elinor's talk with Col. Brandon

She didn't really get into it

She was "... wholly dispirited ... and seeming equally indifferent whether she went or stayed..."[9]

Sense and Sensibility, Volume the Second, Chapter 6, Narrator on Marianne and Lady Middleton's party

Everything's going wrong

"... every circumstance that could embitter such an evil seemed uniting to heighten the misery..."[9]

Sense and Sensibility, Volume the Second, Chapter 6, Narrator on Marianne after encountering Willoughby

She was flustered

She "... sat in such a general tremour as made her fear it impossible to escape ... notice."[9]

Sense and Sensibility, Volume the Second, Chapter 7, Narrator on Elinor after Marianne received a letter

My bad mood

"...my present forlorn and cheerless gravity..."[9]

Sense and Sensibility, Volume the Second, Chapter 9, Col. Brandon to Elinor in telling Willoughby's past

She was bummed

"Her mind ... settled in a gloomy dejection."[9]

Sense and Sensibility, Volume the Second, Chapter 10, Narrator on Marianne after hearing Col. Brandon's story

It made her sad

It "... preyed ... so much of her spirits..."[9]

Sense and Sensibility, Volume the Second, Chapter 10, Narrator on Marianne after hearing Col. Brandon's story

Make her sadder

"...militate against her own happiness..."[9]

Sense and Sensibility, Volume the Second, Chapter 10, Narrator on Elinor remaining in London

She had a lot on her mind

She was "...much oppressed by a crowd of ideas, widely differing in themselves..."[9]

Sense and Sensibility, Volume the Third, Chapter 9, Narrator on Elinor after speaking with Willoughby

It took her a while to calm down

"... it required several hours to give sedateness to her spirits, or any degree of tranquility to her heart."[9]

Sense and Sensibility, Volume the Third, Chapter 13, Narrator on Elinor after Edward's proposal

She was obviously upset

She "... was at no pains to conceal her vexation under the disappointment, or repress the peevishness of her temper-."[3]

The Watsons, Narrator on Margaret when Tom Musgrave did not show for dinner

Chill out

".. soften the evident vexation..."[3]

The Watsons, Narrator on Emma breaking up the argument between Robert & his wife

He's positive

He is "... of a sanguine turn of mind..."[3]

Sanditon, Chapter 2, Narrator on Mr. Parker

With strong emotion

"... in the sublimities of intense feeling..."[3]

Sanditon, Chapter 8, Sir Edward to Charlotte about his tastes in books

The bad mixed in with the good

"... the disadvantages which threatened alloy to her many enjoyments."[1]

Emma, Chapter 1, Narrator's description of Emma Woodhouse.

He was conflicted

His "...feelings were in sad warfare..."[1]

Emma, Chapter 3, Narrator on Mr. Woodhouse at the dinner party

Life has its ups and downs

"... if things are going untowardly one month, they are sure to mend the next."[1]

Emma, Chapter 36, Mr. Weston to Mrs. Elton about Frank returning

Offensive to her

"... so repugnant to her feelings..."[10]

Catherine, Narrator on Cecilia's move to the East Indies

She was a buzz-kill

She "... was a restraint on the vivacity of her companions."[10]
Catherine, Narrator on Mrs. Percival on the way home from the ball

With a strange seriousness

"...with a very unusual solemnity of countenance..."[3]
Lady Susan, Chapter 22, Lady Susan to Mrs. Johnson about Mr. De Courcy

It doesn't bother me

"I am undismayed..."[3]
Lady Susan, Chapter 33, Lady Susan Vernon to Mrs. Johnson about Mrs. Johnson not being home

I just don't care anymore

"... I degenerate into negligence and indifference."[2]
Jane Austen in a letter to Cassandra, Sunday, January 25, 1801, about letter writing

It's not so bad

"... there is certainly not much to try the patience or hurt the Spirits..."[2]
Jane Austen in a letter to Cassandra, Monday, June 20, 1808, about the children at Godmersham

Serious moments

"... situations in which very high spirits would denote insensibility."[5]
Mansfield Park, Chapter 10, Maria to Henry Crawford, comparing her nature to Julia's

It's funny

"... it will be the ruin of all my solemnity."[5]
Mansfield Park, Chapter 14, Henry Crawford to the party on Julia playing the part of Agatha

To make her emotional

To "... exercise her tender enthusiasm..."5
Mansfield Park, Chapter 29, Narrator on Fanny the day after the ball

To play it cool in front of other people

"... to bury the tumult of her feelings under the restraint of society..."5
Mansfield Park, Chapter 20, Narrator on Maria when Henry Crawford announced his leaving for Bath

She was herself again

"... she could afterwards bring her mind without much effort into its everyday state..."5
Mansfield Park, Chapter 29, Narrator on Fanny after visiting the Parsonage

Calm down

"For the present you have only to tranquillize yourself."5
Mansfield Park, Chapter 32, Sir Thomas to Fanny after her refusal of Henry Crawford

Pull yourself together

"... endeavor to reason yourself into a stronger frame of mind."5
Mansfield Park, Chapter 32, Sir Thomas to Fanny after her refusal of Henry Crawford

It started to sink in

"... every moment was quickening her perception of the horrible evil."5
Mansfield Park, Chapter 46, Narrator on Fanny considering Maria's scandal

She seemed just fine

"… no one, observing her … would have supposed she had any wretchedness about her."[6]
Northanger Abbey, Chapter 12, Narrator on Catherine watching the play

She calmed down

"… the flutter of her spirits subsided…"[6]
Northanger Abbey, Chapter 13, Narrator on Catherine after securing her walk with the Tilneys

Not really into it

"A something of languid indifference…"[6]
Northanger Abbey, Chapter 19, Narrator on Isabella's behavior

She finally relaxed

She "… would contend no longer against comfort."[6]
Northanger Abbey, Chapter 19, Narrator on Catherine's concerns about Isabella & Captain Tilney

He couldn't keep a straight face

"… he could no longer command solemnity…"[6]
Northanger Abbey, Chapter 20, Narrator on Mr. Tilney during the ride to Northanger Abbey

She was in a good mood

"… a sense of general happiness preponderated…"[6]
Northanger Abbey, Chapter 21, Narrator on Catherine's first evening at Northanger Abbey

She felt better

"… her spirits were gradually raised to a modest tranquility."[6]
Northanger Abbey, Chapter 25, Narrator on Catherine, the evening after being caught by Mr. Tilney

She was mostly happy

"… she had moments only of languor and depression to hours of occupation and enjoyment."[7]
Persuasion, Chapter 17, Narrator on Mrs. Smith's circumstances

Nothing helped her mood

"Her dejection had no abatement from anything passing around her…"[5]
Mansfield Park, Chapter 42, Narrator on Fanny at home after Henry Crawford left

His mood changed

"The difference between his present air and what it had been … was strikingly great."[7]
Persuasion, Chapter 20, Narrator on the change in Wentworth at the concert

Communication 1

Telling & Receiving News

She shocked her family with the news

She "... imparted no small degree of surprise to her relations..."[8]

Pride and Prejudice, Chapter 44, Narrator on Elizabeth telling the Gardiners about the invitation to meet Georgiana Darcy

Fine, I'll tell you

"...to avoid the imputation of obstinacy or ill-nature, I will gratify the curiosity..."[10]

Love and Friendship, Letter 2nd, Laura to Isabel, agreeing to tell her story to Marianne

Tell him what we decided

"... impart to him the result of our deliberations -."[10]

Love and Friendship, Letter 10th, Laura to Marianne about telling Edward what to do about Augustus

That sounds awesome

"Well, I am prodigiously happy to hear such pleasing news..."[10]

Catherine, Mrs. Stanley to Camilla about Augusta Barlow's dress

I swear. I'm not lying

"Be assured that I speak from the fullest conviction of the truth of what I say..."[3]

Lady Susan, Chapter 23, Mrs. Vernon to Lady De Courcy about Lady Susan wanting Sir James to Marry Frederica

I'm curious how it all went down

"I am all impatience to hear how this
astonishing change was effected."[3]
Lady Susan, Chapter 23, Mrs. Vernon to Lady De Courcy about Lady
Susan's separation from Sir Reginald

I am disturbed by this news

"This eclaircissement is rather provoking."[3]
Lady Susan, Chapter 33, Lady Susan Vernon to Mrs. Johnson about
Mrs. Mainwaring & Mr. Johnson meeting

You know what I'm talking about

"You cannot doubt to what I allude."[3]
Lady Susan, Chapter 34, Mr. De Courcy to Lady Susan about his
learning her real character

That having been said...

"After this necessary preamble I shall proceed to
inform you that..."[2]
Jane Austen in a letter to Cassandra, Saturday, January 9, 1796, telling
about a ball

Tell me all about it

"I shall be extremely anxious ... to receive so
long & minute an account of every particular..."[2]
Jane Austen in a letter to Cassandra, Monday, September 5, 1796, about
a ball Cassandra attended

"... I am impatient for a thousand particulars."[1]
Emma, Chapter 50, Frank in a letter to Mrs. Weston, about her visit to
Jane

Here's the scoop

Here is "A short and compendious history..."[2]
Jane Austen in a letter to Cassandra, Sunday, November 25, 1798,
referring to information about Miss Debary

I hate being the bearer of bad news

"To make long sentences upon unpleasant subjects is very odious..."[2]
Jane Austen in a letter to Cassandra, Thursday, May 21, 1801, before telling her about the Bath housing situation

We know all about it

"We are all quite familiarized to the idea..."[2]
Jane Austen in a letter to Cassandra, Monday, October 24, 1808, about a proposed move to Southampton

I can tell you every little detail

"I can now answer your question ... with equal perspicuity & minuteness..."[2]
Jane Austen in a letter to Cassandra, Tuesday, January 10, 1809, about leaving Southampton

I told you everything

"... I seem rather to have exhausted than spared the subject."[2]
Jane Austen in a letter to Cassandra, Thursday, April 25, 1811, about a large party she attended

I'll find out

"... I am sure of getting the intelligence I want..."[2]
Jane Austen in a letter to Martha Lloyd, Tuesday, February 16, 1813, about getting an update from Henry on Northamptonshire

Now for the bad news

"To vary the subject from Gay to Grave with inimitable address I shall now tell you..."[2]
Jane Austen in a letter to Cassandra, Wednesday, November 3, 1813, changing the subject to Bath

She couldn't keep the secret

She "... talked of it everywhere as a matter not to be talked of at present."[5]
Mansfield Park, Chapter 4, Narrator on Mrs. Norris talking about Maria & Mr. Rushworth's engagement

Bad news

"... distressing communication..."[7]
Persuasion, Chapter 12, Narrator on the news of Louisa's accident

She told what she had witnessed

She "... concluded a short recapitulation of what she had suffered herself by observing..."[7]
Persuasion, Chapter 14, Narrator on Mrs. Musgrove talking with Anne

I get it

"... I have a perfect impression of the general meaning."[7]
Persuasion, Chapter 21, Mrs. Smith on Mr. Elliot's letter to Mr. Smith

Believe me

"... I can give as authentic oral testimony as you can desire..."[7]
Persuasion, Chapter 21, Mrs. Smith on Mr. Elliot

They got all the gossip

"Their visits... were now productive of the most interesting intelligence."[8]
Pride and Prejudice, Chapter 7, Narrator on Catherine's & Lydia's visits to Mrs. Philips

What were you thinking?

"... what ideas have you been admitting?"[6]
Northanger Abbey, Chapter 24, Mr. Tilney to Catherine on her surmises of Mrs. Tilney's fate

She gave them the bad news

"To the civil enquiries which poured in ... she could not make a very favourable answer."[8]
Pride and Prejudice, Chapter 8, Narrator on Elizabeth's report of Jane's condition

Popular gossip

"... affairs which... were treated as of such general publicity and pervading interest..."[7]
Persuasion, Chapter 6, Narrator on Anne's visit to Uppercross

We got to know the real her

"... the mask she had so long supported was by degrees thrown aside..."[4]
Lesley Castle, Margaret to Charlotte on Louisa after marrying

Glad to hear it

"You rejoice me by what you say..."[2]
Jane Austen in a letter to Cassandra, Tuesday, January 24, 1809, about the news about Fanny

Rumors

"... the reports beginning to prevail."[7]
Persuasion, Chapter 21, Mrs. Smith on Mrs. Clay's designs on Sir Walter

She couldn't wait to spill the beans

She had "... such a temptation to openness as nothing could have conquered..."[8]
Pride and Prejudice, Chapter 38, Narrator on Elizabeth's desire to tell Jane what had happened at Hunsford

He spilled the beans

"His was an involuntary confidence, an irrepressible effusion..."[9]
Sense and Sensibility, Volume the Third, Chapter 9, Mrs. Dashwood to Elinor about Col. Brandon's confessed attachment

She talked about her day

She "… was enumerating the various pleasures of the morning to any body who would hear her."[8]

Pride and Prejudice, Chapter 39, Narrator on Lydia

Talking about it made her feel better

Her "… tumult of … mind was allayed by … conversation."[8]

Pride and Prejudice, Chapter 40, Narrator Elizabeth telling Jane about Mr. Darcy's letter

Happy to talk about it

"… brought forward and dwelt upon with so rapturous a delight…"[9]

Sense and Sensibility, Volume the First, Chapter 10, Narrator on Marianne's favorite subjects

He listened closely

"He heard her with the most earnest attention…"[9]

Sense and Sensibility, Volume the Second, Chapter 4, Narrator on Col. Brandon listening to Elinor

She gave the short version

"… she confined herself to the brief repetition of such simple particulars…"[9]

Sense and Sensibility, Volume the Third, Chapter 2, Narrator on Elinor telling Mrs. Jennings what Anne Steele had heard

She was distracted by his talking

She "… was too intent on what he said to pursue her employment."[9]

Sense and Sensibility, Volume the Third, Chapter 3, Narrator on Elinor listening to Col. Brandon

What good news!

"... the relief of such tidings was very great..."[1]
Emma, Chapter 15, Narrator on Mr. Knightley reporting the condition of the roads

Digging for nasty gossip

"... with the insidious design of further discovery..."[1]
Emma, Chapter 19, Narrator on Emma wanting to know more about Jane Fairfax & Mr. Dixon

Please explain

"... make this intelligible to me."[1]
Emma, Chapter 54, Emma to Mr. Knightley about Harriet's engagement to Robert Martin

His word is not enough

His word "...is not of such potent intelligence as to supersede the necessity of more."[3]
Lady Susan, Chapter 35, Lady Susan to Mr. De Courcy about Langford

You never know

"...I do not see how it can ever be ascertained..."[3]
Lady Susan, Conclusion, Narrator to Reader

He had a right to know

"... he was not proceeding beyond a very allowable curiosity."[5]
Mansfield Park, Chapter 19, Narrator on Sir Thomas inquiring about the billiard table

She liked to talk about it

She "... could not but indulge herself in dwelling on so beloved a theme."[5]
Mansfield Park, Chapter 43, Narrator on Fanny talking to Susan about Mansfield Park

I'll give her your excuses

"I will tell her all that is necessary to what may comparatively be called your justification."[9]
Sense and Sensibility, Volume the Third, Chapter 8, Elinor to Willoughby about speaking to Marianne

Manner of Talk/Communication

Good writing

Where "... the liveliest effusions of wit and humour are conveyed to the world in the best chosen language."[6]
Northanger Abbey, Chapter 5, Narrator on novels

To harshly scold

"... to upbraid ... in such opprobrious language..."[10]
Love and Friendship, Letter 13th, Laura to Marianne about Macdonald walking in on Sophia stealing

She gave a mean look

Her "... looks were by no means calculated to animate the spirits..."[10]
Catherine, Narrator on Mrs. Percival approaching Catherine in the arbour

You seem certain

"You speak with such noble resignation..."[2]
Jane Austen in a letter to Cassandra, Thursday, January 8, 1801, about Mrs. Jordan & the Opera House

That was random

You spoke "... in a loose, disultary, unconnected strain..."[2]
Jane Austen in a letter to Martha Lloyd, Wednesday, November 12, 1800, about repeating Henry's History of England

I digress

"I shall now try to say only what is necessary, I am weary of meandering..."[2]
Jane Austen in a letter to Cassandra, Monday, January 30, 1809, about Jane's criticism of the 1809 Hannah More novel *Coelebs in Search of a Wife*[1]

"... I seem to be spinning out of my story to an endless length."[3]
Sanditon, Chapter 9, Diana Parker to Mr. Parker in telling of the West Indies party

He speaks with passion

He is "... a little too eager sometimes in his delivery, but that is to me a better extreme than the want of animation, especially when it evidently comes from the heart as in him."[2]
Jane Austen in a letter to Frank, Saturday, September 25, 1813, about Mr. Sherer's sermon

He wasn't very tactful

He "... addressed them ... with rather an injudicious particularity."[5]
Mansfield Park, Chapter 2, Narrator on Sir Thomas' communications with his daughters

She was curt

"... her answers were as short and indifferent as civility allowed."[5]
Mansfield Park, Chapter 23, Narrator on Fanny being questioned by Henry Crawford

His fast talking

"… his rapidity of expression…"[6]
Northanger Abbey, Chapter 9, Narrator on John Thorpe's speech to Catherine

She started babbling

"… there was then an opportunity … to utter some few of the many thousand things which had been collecting within her for communication…"[6]
Northanger Abbey, Chapter 10, Narrator on Isabella speaking to Catherine

She was very vocal

She "… was profuse in her acknowledgements."[8]
Pride and Prejudice, Chapter 9, Narrator on Mrs. Bennet praising Mr. Bingley

He was honest and polite

He was "… unaffectedly civil in his answer…"[8]
Pride and Prejudice, Chapter 9, Narrator on Mr. Bingley's response to Mrs. Bennet's gratitude

He had a way with words

"… the commonest, dullest, most threadbare topic might be rendered interesting by the skill of the speaker."[8]
Pride and Prejudice, Chapter 16, Narrator on Mr. Wickham talking about the weather

She wouldn't shut up

"… she was a most determined talker…"[8]
Pride and Prejudice, Chapter 16, Narrator on Lydia

He could tell she meant it

"…the sincerity of her manner being soon sufficient to convince him…"[7]
Persuasion, Chapter 7, Narrator on Anne

You sound bitter

"…that speech savours strongly of disappointment."[8]
Pride and Prejudice, Chapter 27, Mrs. Gardiner to Elizabeth on her comments about men

Her conceited yammering

"…delivering her opinion on every subject in so decisive a manner as proved that she was not used to have her judgment controverted."[8]
Pride and Prejudice, Chapter 29, Narrator on Lady Catherine's discourse

Rudely

"… with so little endeavour at civility.."[8]
Pride and Prejudice, Chapter 34, Narrator on Mr. Darcy's reaction to Elizabeth's reply to his proposal

Painfully honest

"… in terms of such mortifying, yet merited reproach…"[8]
Pride and Prejudice, Chapter 36, Narrator on Mr. Darcy's account of the Bennet's behavior

That is what they kept whining about

"Such were the kind of lamentations resounding perpetually…"[8]
Pride and Prejudice, Chapter 41, Narrator on Mrs. Bennet & the younger girls missing the regiment

To speak freely

"… to engage … in unreserved conversation."[9]
Sense and Sensibility, Volume the First, Chapter 4, Elinor to Marianne on Edward Ferrars

Loud yelling

"...such violent screams, as could hardly be outdone by any creature professedly noisy."[9]
Sense and Sensibility, Volume the First, Chapter 21, Narrator on Annamaria after being scratched by a pin

"...in a voice so little attempting concealment..."[9]
Sense and Sensibility, Volume the Second, Chapter 8, Col. Brandon to Elinor on hearing about Willoughby's engagement

She whispered

She "... confined herself to this silent ejaculation..."[9]
Sense and Sensibility, Volume the Third, Chapter 3, Narrator on Mrs. Jennings' response to overhearing Col. Brandon

I'm not good at telling stories

"You will find me a very awkward narrator..."[9]
Sense and Sensibility, Volume the Second, Chapter 9, Col. Brandon to Elinor in telling Willoughby's past

To flatter her

"... to gratify her vanity and raise her self-importance..."[9]
Sense and Sensibility, Volume the Third, Chapter 5, Narrator on Elinor in conversation with John Dashwood

Pretending to care

"... said ... with mock solemnity."[5]
Mansfield Park, Chapter 18, Narrator on Mrs. Grant declaring that Dr. Grant is ill

He stared at her

"He...eyed her fixedly."[5]
Mansfield Park, Chapter 32, Narrator on Sir Thomas' reaction to Fanny's refusal of Henry Crawford

She was being honest

"All this was said, and with the earnestness of sincerity..."[5]
Mansfield Park, Chapter 33, Narrator on Fanny's insistence that she did not love Henry Crawford

She was too easy on him

"Her manner was incurably gentle; and she was not aware of how much it concealed the sternness of her purpose."[5]
Mansfield Park, Chapter 33, Narrator on Fanny's insistence that she did not love Henry Crawford

She was a sucker for kind words

"Her disposition was peculiarly calculated to value a fond treatment..."[5]
Mansfield Park, Chapter 36, Narrator on Fanny's inability to refuse Mary Crawford

We're just humoring them

"Our approbation ... is bur eleemosynary."[3]
Sanditon, Chapter 8, Sir Edward to Charlotte about antagonist characters in novels

Trendiness

"... the common rate of social intercourse..."[1]
Emma, Chapter 11, Narrator on John Knighley preferring to stay at home

Communication 2

Light Talk & Keeping in Touch

Writing back and forth

"...epistolary intercourse..."[3]
Lady Susan, Conclusion, Narrator to Reader

I'll keep in touch

I am "... determined that the Correspondence should never cease thro' my means."[2]

I expect people to write to me

"My ideas of Justice in Epistolary Matters are you know very strict."[2]
Jane Austen in a letter to Martha Lloyd, Tuesday, February 16, 1813, about deserving a letter

Light chat

"... we talked away at a great rate about nothing worth hearing."[2]
Jane Austen in a letter to Cassandra, Monday, October 11, 1813, about Mr. Chisholme

"A great deal of goodhumoured pleasantry..."[3]
The Watsons, Narrator on the Edwardses & Emma after the assembly

It's your turn to write to me

"... I believe the Epistolary debt is on your side..."[2]
Jane Austen in a letter to Miss Bigg, Friday, January 24, 1817

I came to love our talks

Our "... daily intercourse had become precious by habit."[7]
Persuasion, Chapter 5, Narrator on Anne leaving Lady Russell

Talking 'glory days'

"... remembering former partialities and talking over old times."[7]
Persuasion, Chapter 17, Narrator on Anne's visit to Mrs. Smith

Blabbing

"... engaging ... in incessant conversation..."[1]
Emma, Chapter 10, Narrator on Emma with Mr. Elton's servant

Light, friendly talk

"... mere lively chat, such as any young persons, on an intimate footing, might fall into."[7]
Persuasion, Chapter 10, Narrator on Wentworth's conversation with the Miss Musgroves

They made small talk

"Mutual enquiries on common subjects passed..."[7]
Persuasion, Chapter 19, Narrator on Anne's first encounter with Wentworth in Bath

We'll talk soon

"... we will hope at some future period, to enjoy many returns of the delightful intercourse we have known..."[8]
Pride and Prejudice, Chapter 21, Caroline Bingley in a letter to Jane on leaving Netherfield for London

We'll write to each other

We "... may lessen the pain of separation by a very frequent and most unreserved correspondence."[8]

Pride and Prejudice, Chapter 21, Caroline Bingley in a letter to Jane on leaving Netherfield for London

They talked about a lot of things

"... various were the subjects which occupied them..."[8]

Pride and Prejudice, Chapter 39, Narrator on the conversations upon Elizabeth's return to Longbourn

Stuff to talk about

"...provision for discourse."[9]

Sense and Sensibility, Volume the First, Chapter 6, Narrator on bringing children to a visit

Plain talk

Expressions "... unadorned ... by any such broad wreath of gallantry..."[1]

Emma, Chapter 31, Narrator on Frank's letter to Mrs. Weston after his return to Enscombe

She was a motor mouth

"She was a great talker upon little matters..."[1]

Emma, Chapter 3, Narrator on Miss Bates

Not Communicating/Not Listening

I had to bite my lip…hard

"It was the greatest stretch of forbearance I could practise."[3]
Lady Susan, Chapter 24, Mrs. Vernon to Lady De Courcy

Don't listen to gossip

"To be guided by second hand conjecture is pitiful."[6]
Northanger Abbey, Chapter 19, Mr. Tilney to Catherine her worries for James

Hard to explain

"… too great for any endeavor at discourse…"[6]
Northanger Abbey, Chapter 24, Narrator on Catherine's agitation as Eleanor took her to the great gallery

They're too shy

"… they do not talk freely enough to be agreable…"[2]
Jane Austen in a letter to Cassandra, Saturday, October 1, 1808, about the Miss Ballards

She held her tongue

"She restrained herself … from any of the reproofs she could have given…"[1]
Emma, Chapter 32, Narrator on Emma in conversation with Mrs. Elton

She "… heard it in silent indignation."[8]
Pride and Prejudice, Chapter 24, Narrator on Elizabeth hearing Caroline Bingley's letter

"…it was highly incumbent on her to clothe her imagination, her memory, and all her ideas…"[7]
Persuasion, Chapter 6, Narrator on Anne's visit to Uppercross

"The complaints and lamentations which politeness had hitherto restrained..."[9]
Sense and Sensibility, Volume the First, Chapter 13, Narrator on the Whitwell party's disappointment

"...how much more might have been said but for the restraints of propriety."[1]
Emma, Chapter 31, Narrator on Frank's letter to Mrs. Weston after his return to Enscombe

I am speechless

"I will not attempt to describe my astonishment..."[3]
Lady Susan, Chapter 35, Lady Susan to Mr. De Courcy about the note she received from him

"I ... could not frame a sentence."[9]
Sense and Sensibility, Volume the Third, Chapter 8, Willoughby to Elinor explaining his behavior

She wouldn't speak too soon

"...she would venture on little more than hints of what might be hereafter..."[7]
Persuasion, Chapter 17, Narrator on Lady Russell's intimations of Mr. Elliot's intentions

It was hard for her to talk about her problems

The "... suffering of her situation, had been such as could not be related without anguish of spirit..."[7]
Persuasion, Chapter 21, Narrator on Mrs. Smith

Let her believe whatever she wants

"I do not endeavor to undeceive her…"[2]
Jane Austen in a letter to Cassandra, Tuesday, January 24, 1809, about Martha & her influence

She doesn't want to talk about it

"… it may well be a disagreable subject to her…"[2]
Jane Austen in a letter to Cassandra, Tuesday, December 28, 1808, about Mary & the garden

She "… would not vouchsafe an answer."[9]
Sense and Sensibility, Volume the Second, Chapter 11, Narrator on Elinor's conversation with John Dashwood

She couldn't flatter

She had "… an inability of administering to the vanity of others…"[6]
Northanger Abbey, Chapter 14, Narrator

We don't talk about it

"… not a syllable of that nature is ever breathed."[2]
Jane Austen in a letter to Cassandra, Tuesday, October 12, 1813, about Mrs. Frank Austen & children visiting

"…make no enquiries on so prohibited a subject…"[9]
Sense and Sensibility, Volume the Third, Chapter 11, John Dashwood in a letter to Elinor about Edward Ferrars

He was tired of his wife's talking

He was "… fatigued with the raptures of his wife."[8]
Pride and Prejudice, Chapter 2, Narrator on Mr. Bennet

She couldn't express her feelings

"...there were emotions of tenderness that could not be clothed in words."[5]
Mansfield Park, Chapter 37, Narrator on Fanny's return to Portsmouth with William

Her "...feelings, though fervent, were little displayed..."[8]
Pride and Prejudice, Chapter 36, Narrator on Jane's behavior around Mr. Bingley

We're both quiet loners

"We are each of an unsocial, taciturn disposition..."[8]
Pride and Prejudice, Chapter 18, Elizabeth to Mr. Darcy

The cold shoulder

"... stiffness of manner and resentful silence."[8]
Pride and Prejudice, Chapter 21, Narrator on Mr. Collins after being refused by Elizabeth

He didn't care what she had to say

He had "...a calm unconcern which was not in the least altered by her communication."[8]
Pride and Prejudice, Chapter 20, Narrator on Mr. Bennet's reaction to Mrs. Bennet and Elizabeth's refusal of Mr. Collins

Mum's the word

"... the subject was never alluded to."[8]
Pride and Prejudice, Chapter 23, Narrator on Mr. Bingley's continued absence from Netherfield

You won't hear me whining

"But I will not repine."[8]
Pride and Prejudice, Chapter 24, Jane to Elizabeth about the loss of Mr. Bingley

She gave him the cold shoulder

"She answered him with cold civility."[8]
Pride and Prejudice, Chapter 34, Narrator on Elizabeth's reply to Mr. Darcy's enquiries

Is that all you have to say?

"And this is all the reply which I am to have the honour of expecting!"[8]
Pride and Prejudice, Chapter 34, Narrator on Mr. Darcy's reaction to Elizabeth's reply to his proposal

He wanted to keep his plan a secret

He "...forbade the slightest hint being dropped of his having such an intention..."[7]
Persuasion, Chapter 2, Narrator on Sir Walter

Someone who doesn't answer his phone or return texts

"... a most negligent and dilatory correspondent..."[8]
Pride and Prejudice, Chapter 48, Narrator on Mr. Bennet

She had a secret she couldn't tell

"But there was still something lurking behind, of which prudence forbad the disclosure."[8]
Pride and Prejudice, Chapter 40, Narrator Elizabeth not telling Jane about Mr. Bingley

"... nothing ... could justify her in throwing off this last encumbrance of mystery."[8]
Pride and Prejudice, Chapter 40, Narrator Elizabeth not telling Jane about Mr. Bingley

He was discreet

"There were few people on whose secrecy she would have more confidently depended..."[8]
Pride and Prejudice, Chapter 50, Narrator on Elizabeth's confidence in Mr. Darcy's discretion

Too coy

"...the restraint of sentiments which were not in themselves illaudable..."[9]
Sense and Sensibility, Volume the First, Chapter 11, Narrator on Marianne defending her flirting

Tight-lipped

"...deficient ... in a disposition to communicate..."[9]
Sense and Sensibility, Volume the First, Chapter 21, Narrator on Elinor's thought of Mrs. Jennings

She didn't want to talk

She "... entreated her, with all the eagerness of the most nervous irritability, not to speak to her for the world."[9]
Sense and Sensibility, Volume the Second, Chapter 7, Narrator on Marianne & Elinor

I don't like to talk about it

"On such a subject ... I can have little temptation to be diffuse."[9]
Sense and Sensibility, Volume the Second, Chapter 9, Col. Brandon to Elinor in telling Willoughby's past

It shut them up

It "...made farther conversation most thoroughly undesirable."[3]
The Watsons, Narrator on the noise as Emma & Elizabeth entered the turnpike

No time for such chit-chat

"...time not allowing for the circuitous train of intelligence which had been hitherto kept up..."[3]
Sanditon, Chapter 10, Narrator on Diana Parker's note to Mrs. Griffiths

Introverted

"...such extreme and perpetual cautiousness of word and manner..."[1]
Emma, Chapter 24, Emma to Frank about Jane

Everybody ignored her

She "...was wanting notice, which nobody had inclination to pay..."[1]
Emma, Chapter 36, Narrator on Mrs. Elton at the Hartfield dinner party

I can't be fake

"...I never had the convenient talent of affecting sensations foreign to my heart..."[3]
Lady Susan, Chapter 20, Mrs. Vernon to Lady De Courcy

They don't understand us

Their "...sensibilities are not of a nature to comprehend ours."[3]
Lady Susan, Chapter 30, Lady Susan Vernon to Mr. De Courcy about Mrs. Vernon

Nobody cared what she thought

"Few ... could be less called on to speak their opinion..."[5]
Mansfield Park, Chapter 5, Narrator on Fanny's opinion of the Crawfords

Staying out of it

"... unwilling to exasperate ... by interference..."[5]
Mansfield Park, Chapter 15, Narrator on Edmund not supporting Fanny

She has no answer

She is "... proving incompetent to suggest any reply..."[5]
Mansfield Park, Chapter 16, Narrator on Fanny's attic room being of no help to her

She wasn't really interested

Her "... curiosity did not appear of that absorbing nature as wholly to occupy her."[1]

Emma, Chapter 21, Narrator on Jane's interest in Mr. Elton's marriage

Being a hermit

"... drawing back from intimacies in general, ... particularly disinclined ... for any engagements..."[5]

Mansfield Park, Chapter 21, Narrator on Sir Thomas after his return from Antigua

I can't make up my mind

"My feelings are at present in a state of dreadful indecision..."[9]

Sense and Sensibility, Volume the Second, Chapter 7, Marianne in a letter to Willoughby

Don't mention it

"Such a trifle is not worth half so many words"[5]

Mansfield Park, Chapter 26, Mary Crawford to Fanny about accepting the gold necklace

She couldn't defend him

"... she had not a syllable to say for him."[1]

Emma, Chapter 52, Narrator on Emma not accounting for Mr. Knightley missing his appointment with Mr. Elton

Don't tease

"... what could excuse the use of such words ... if they meant but to trifle?"[5]

Mansfield Park, Chapter 31, Narrator on Henry Crawford's proposal to Fanny

Let me know if you are not feeling well

"...I hope you will not be cruelly concealing any tendency to indisposition."[5]
Mansfield Park, Chapter 42, Henry Crawford to Fanny on his readiness to return her to Mansfield

Miscellaneous Communication

Making no excuses

"...without even endeavoring to exculpate himself..."[10]
Love and Friendship, Letter 13th, Laura to Marianne about Macdonald walking in on Sophia

To tell you the truth ...

"I will not disguise my sentiments ... from you..."[3]
Lady Susan, Chapter 8, Mrs. Vernon to Lady De Courcy

I tried to warn you

"I ...imparted my apprehensions to you..."[3]
Lady Susan, Chapter 23, Mrs. Vernon to Lady De Courcy

You understand me

"...you will scarcely affect further wonder at my meaning..."[3]
Lady Susan, Chapter 36, Mr. De Courcy to Lady Susan about consoling Mrs. Mainwaring

I had to vent

"Having now relieved my heart of a great deal of malevolence..."[2]
Jane Austen in a letter to Cassandra, Sunday, November 25, 1798, Jane complaining that Cassandra hadn't written

You're preaching to the choir

"It is rather impertinent to suggest any household care to a housekeeper..."[2]
Jane Austen in a letter to Cassandra, Tuesday, June 11, 1799, about Edward drinking coffee for breakfast

She couldn't bite her tongue

"...her feelings found a rapid vent."[8]
Pride and Prejudice, Chapter 23, Narrator on Mrs. Bennet's reaction to Charlotte's engagement

They had a good debate

"The greatest degree of rational consistency could not have been more engaging..."[5]
Mansfield Park, Chapter 9, Narrator on Edmund & Mary Crawford arguing the distance of the Sotherton lane

Change the subject

"...turn the current of ... ideas into a happier channel."[5]
Mansfield Park, Chapter 20, Narrator on Mrs. Norris in conversation with Sir Thomas

They're going to tease me

"...they will quiz me famously."[6]
Northanger Abbey, Chapter 10, John Thorpe to Catherine about losing his dance with her

She didn't make much sense

"The business ... [was] not perfectly elucidated by this speech..."[6]
Northanger Abbey, Chapter 13, Narrator on Catherine's excuse to the Tilneys

She didn't get it

"...she listened to them with an attention which brought her little profit, for they talked in phrases which conveyed scarcely any idea to her."[6]
Northanger Abbey, Chapter 14, Narrator on Catherine's walk with the Tilneys

Shouting out ideas

"...forming wise resolutions with the most violent dispatch."[6]
Northanger Abbey, Chapter 21, Narrator on Catherine after being caught searching the chest

Just say "no"

Have an "... opposing desire that should dare to clothe itself in words..."[6]
Northanger Abbey, Chapter 30, Narrator on Mr. Tilney arguing with his father

He didn't approve, but no one cared

"His disapprobation was expressed, but apparently very little regarded."[7]
Persuasion, Chapter 1, Narrator on Sir Walter and Mr. Elliot

She had to hear him out

"...she had to encounter all the additional pain of opinions, on his side..."[7]
Persuasion, Chapter 4, Narrator on Anne hearing Wentworth's protests to the broken engagement

You can say what you want

"Oh! I lay no embargo on anybody's words."[7]
Persuasion, Chapter 22, Elizabeth to Mrs. Clay

Huh? What are you talking about?

"What can be the meaning of that emphatic exclamation?"[8]

Pride and Prejudice, Chapter 2, Mr. Bennet to Mrs. Bennet

Are you just humoring me?

"Are you consulting your own feelings in the present case, or do you imagine that you are gratifying mine?"[8]

Pride and Prejudice, Chapter 18, Mr. Darcy to Elizabeth on the need to talk while dancing

She moved on to pleasanter topics

"She then changed the discourse to one more gratifying to each..."[8]

Pride and Prejudice, Chapter 18, Narrator on Elizabeth & Jane talking of Mr. Wickham

Can I talk to you alone?

May "...I solicit for the honor of a private audience...?"[8]

Pride and Prejudice, Chapter 19, Mr. Collins to Mrs. Bennet, requesting to speak to Elizabeth

You know what I'm about to say

"You can hardly doubt the purport of my discourse..."[8]

Pride and Prejudice, Chapter 19, Mr. Collins to Elizabeth

She was her same, complaining self again

She "...was restored to her usual querulous serenity..."[8]

Pride and Prejudice, Chapter 41, Narrator on Mrs. Bennet

Attempt to start a conversation

"...endeavour to introduce some kind of discourse..."[8]

Pride and Prejudice, Chapter 45, Narrator on Mrs. Annesley at Pemberley

She hogged his attention

She "... secured the largest share of his discourse to herself..."[9]

Sense and Sensibility, Volume the First, Chapter 10, Narrator on Marianne with Willoughby

Chattiness

"... hours spent in the hard labour of incessant talking..."[9]

Sense and Sensibility, Volume the Third, Chapter 13, Narrator on Elinor & Edward after Edward's proposal

With a serious look

"...expressing with a most intelligent portentous countenance..."[3]

Sanditon, Chapter 1, Narrator Mr. Parker's driver turning up the lane

Pray about it

"...commit the event to a higher power."[3]

Lady Susan, Chapter 15, Mrs. Vernon to Lady De Courcy about Reginald's fate

Boredom & Excitement

Boredom

Boring

"…such impenetrable calmness, such dreadful indifference!"[9]
Sense and Sensibility, Volume the First, Chapter 3, Marianne to Mrs. Dashwood on Edward Ferrars' reading

"…it produced not one novelty of thought or expression…"[9]
Sense and Sensibility, Volume the Second, Chapter 1, Narrator on Elinor's evening with Lady Middleton

Bored

"…wanting to be again in scenes of agitation & exertion."[2]
Jane Austen in a letter to Cassandra, Thursday, February 4, 1813, about Martha

"…having so much leisure as to make almost any novelty a certain good…"[5]
Mansfield Park, Chapter 13, Narrator on Thomas when the play was suggested

Bored and lonely

"…suffering an hour's ennui, from the want of her companionableness…"[1]
Emma, Chapter 2, Narrator on Mrs. Weston's fears for Emma

There was nothing new to think about

"No … importation of novelties could enrich their intellectual stores at present."[1]
Emma, Chapter 42, Narrator on the Sucklings not visiting until autumn

He bored me silly

"My spirits are quite jaded with listening to his nonsense..."[6]
Northanger Abbey, Chapter 16, Isabella to Catherine about her dance with Captain Tilney

She was so boring

Her "... cold insipidity ... was so particularly repulsive..."[9]
Sense and Sensibility, Volume the First, Chapter 7, Narrator on Lady Middleton

Her fear of being sad and bored

Her "... vigorous sketch of their future ennui..."[9]
Sense and Sensibility, Volume the Third, Chapter 3, Narrator on Mrs. Jennings telling Col. Brandon about the Miss Dashwoods departure

It's boring there

"... it is the most tiresome place in the world."[6]
Northanger Abbey, Chapter 10, Mr. Tilney to Catherine about a long stay in Bath

Excitement

Excited

"... with spirits elated to rapture..."[6]
Northanger Abbey, Chapter 17, Narrator on Catherine being invited to Northanger Abbey

Exciting

"...so poignant and so ceaseless in interest."[7]
Persuasion, Chapter 23, Narrator on Wentworth and Anne's conversation

More excited than normal

"With an alacrity beyond the common impulse of a spirit..."[1]
Emma, Chapter 3, Narrator on Emma hosting the dinner party

I am too excited to write

"I am so much agitated by delight that I can scarcely hold a pen..."[3]
Lady Susan, Chapter 23, Mrs. Vernon to Lady De Courcy

She was excited

She "... was all eager delight..."[6]
Northanger Abbey, Chapter 2, Narrator on Catherine, about arriving in Bath

"...she called herself without scruple the happiest of mortals."[6]
Northanger Abbey, Chapter 15, Narrator on Isabella upon receiving James' letter

Her "...expectations of pleasure ... were so very high..."[6]
Northanger Abbey, Chapter 16, Narrator on Catherine at dinner with the Tilneys

"... she was every thing by turns but tranquil..."[9]
Sense and Sensibility, Volume the Third, Chapter 13, Narrator on Elinor after Edward's proposal

"...her spirits were by no means insensible to the expected joys..."[3]
The Watsons, Narrator on Emma approaching the Edwardses

"...she enjoyed the thought of it to an extraordinary degree."[1]
Emma, Chapter 30, Narrator on Jane and the ball

I'm so excited

"I am in such extasies at the thoughts..."[6]
Northanger Abbey, Chapter 11, Isabella to Catherine about the ride to Bristol

"...my languor is entirely removed."[2]
Jane Austen in a letter to Cassandra, Wednesday, June 22, 1808

She was excited and talkative

She "… was all delight and volubility…"[5]

Mansfield Park, Chapter 8, Narrator on Mrs. Norris upon seeing Sotherton

They were excited about it

It "… was of material service in recommending it to their lasting approbation."[9]

Sense and Sensibility, Volume the First, Chapter 6, Narrator on the Dashwood's first impression of Barton Cottage

How surprising

"I was most uncommonly shocked, indeed."[9]

Sense and Sensibility, Volume the Third, Chapter 5, Robert Ferrars to Elinor about Edward & Lucy

Anger/Disappointment & Envy

That sucks

"Is not this most vexatious..."[1]
Emma, Chapter 42, Mrs. Elton to Mr. Knightley about having to postpone the Box Hill scheme

"I cannot conceive of a situation more deplorable."[9]
Sense and Sensibility, Volume the Third, Chapter 1, John Dashwood to Mrs. Jennings about Edward Ferrars' disinheritance

"I cannot picture to myself a more wretched condition."[9]
Sense and Sensibility, Volume the Third, Chapter 1, John Dashwood to Mrs. Jennings about Edward Ferrars' disinheritance

"Can anything be more galling to the spirit of a man..."[9]
Sense and Sensibility, Volume the Third, Chapter 1, John Dashwood to Mrs. Jennings about Edward Ferrars' disinheritance

"But it was a heavy blow!"[6]
Northanger Abbey, Chapter 25, James in a letter to Catherine about Isabella's affair with Captain Tilney

She seemed upset by it

She "... had all the evidence of corresponding perturbation."[1]
Emma, Chapter 21, Narrator on Harriet after running into Robert Martin

You could tell he was angry

"... the mixture of pique and pretention now spread over his air."[1]
Emma, Chapter 22, Narrator on Mr. Elton after his engagement

She pissed me off

"I confess myself not equally satisfied with the behaviour of his lady." [3]

Lady Susan, Chapter 5, Lady Susan Vernon to Mrs. Johnson about Mrs. Vernon

That's gotta piss you off

"... well, that must be infinitely provoking!" [1]

Emma, Chapter 36, Mrs. Elton to Mr. Weston about Mrs. Churchill's behavior

He was disgusted

He "... found much to offend his ideas of decorum..." [5]

Mansfield Park, Chapter 19, Narrator on Sir Thomas listening to Mr. Yates talk about the theatre

He was in a bad mood

His "... state might be best defined by the expressive phrase of being out of humor." [1]

Emma, Chapter 42, Narrator on Frank when arrived at Donwell

I was mad!

"... I never remember suffering any vexation equal to what I experienced..." [4]

Lesley Castle, Charlotte to Margaret on wasting the food

... though it pissed them off

... "to the infinite mortification ..." [1]

Emma, Chapter 2, Narrator on Mr. and Mrs. Churchill

I shouldn't have pissed him off

"I am sorry to have incurred his displeasure..." [3]

Lady Susan, Chapter 15, Mrs. Vernon to Lady De Courcy about Mr. De Courcy

He was really mad!

"...he gave way to the most violent indignation..."[3]
Lady Susan, Chapter 22, Lady Susan to Mrs. Johnson about Sir James

I was angry, and with good reason

"...I was, in truth, in high irritation, and with ample cause."[3]
Lady Susan, Chapter 25, Lady Susan to Mrs. Johnson

You shouldn't let it bother you

"It was folly to be disturbed by it."[1]
Emma, Chapter 21, Narrator on Emma hearing of the Martins' good behavior

He seemed to calm down some

"The angry emotions which had marked every feature when we last parted were partially subdued."[3]
Lady Susan, Chapter 25, Lady Susan to Mrs. Johnson

You piss me off

"...you agitate me beyond expression..."[3]
Lady Susan, Chapter 35, Lady Susan to Mr. De Courcy

It's all gone to hell

"...matters have fallen out so unpleasantly..."[2]
Jane Austen in a letter to Cassandra, Thursday January 14, 1796, in response to news from Cassandra

Angry

"... with a strong sense of ill-usage..."[5]
Mansfield Park, Chapter 17, Narrator on Julia's reaction to Henry Crawford's attentions to Maria

Mad about having to give something up

"...ill-used by so forced a relinquishment..."[7]
Persuasion, Chapter 4, Narrator on Wentworth losing Anne

It always bothered her

It "... was a perpetual provocation to her..."[7]
Persuasion, Chapter 16, Narrator on Lady Russell's reaction to the treatment of Anne

She pretended to be angry

She "...was in a very animated, comfortable state of imaginary agitation..."[7]
Persuasion, Chapter 6, Narrator on Mary

Her conceit angers me

"... she does sometimes provoke me excessively by her nonsense and pride..."[7]
Persuasion, Chapter 10, Louisa to Wentworth, about Mary

She held a grudge

"Nor did that day wear out her resentment."[8]
Pride and Prejudice, Chapter 23, Narrator on Mrs. Bennet's reaction to Charlotte's engagement

They were angry beyond words

"... their indignation would hardly have found expression in their united volubility."[8]
Pride and Prejudice, Chapter 41, Narrator on Mrs. Bennet & Lydia about Elizabeth's talk with Mr. Bennet

In angry judgment

With "... invectives against the villainous conduct..."[8]
Pride and Prejudice, Chapter 47, Narrator on Mrs. Bennet's complaints about Mr. Wickham

She could hardly contain her anger

She "… could with difficulty govern her vexation…"[9]

Sense and Sensibility, Volume the Second, Chapter 4, Narrator on Marianne in the London shops

Patience wears thin

"…the greatest degree of forbearance may be overcome…"[3]

Lady Susan, Chapter 22, Lady Susan to Mrs. Johnson

They threw us under the bus

"Such perfidious treachery in the merciless perpetrators of the deed…"[10]

Love and Friendship, Letter 9th, Laura to Marianne about Augustus getting arrested

Bummer!

"It is a grievous business."[1]

Emma, Chapter 11, Mr. Woodhouse to Isabella on Mrs. Weston's marriage

Almost jealous

With "… feelings so near akin to envy…"[5]

Mansfield Park, Chapter 42, Narrator on Fanny thinking about Henry Crawford with Mary & Edmund

She was bitter

"… she regarded her with jealous abhorrence."[8]

Pride and Prejudice, Chapter 23, Narrator on Mrs. Bennet's treatment of Charlotte

Fear, Worry & Doubt

She was worried

"...she could not help feeling dreadful presentiments..."[5]
Mansfield Park, Chapter 4, Narrator on Mrs. Norris' concerns for Sir Thomas' wellbeing in Antigua

Her "...consideration of it did not become less agitated."[5]
Mansfield Park, Chapter 18, Narrator on Fanny watching the rehearsal

She "...was not entirely free from similar apprehensions..."[5]
Mansfield Park, Chapter 4, Narrator on Mary Crawford being satisfied in Mansfield

"...she was often under the influence of much less sanguine views."[5]
Mansfield Park, Chapter 27, Narrator on Fanny's anticipation of the ball

"A thousand alarming presentiments of evil ... must oppress her heart with sadness..."[6]
Northanger Abbey, Chapter 2, Narrator on Mrs. Morland when Catherine left for Bath

She "... worked herself into a state of real distress."[6]
Northanger Abbey, Chapter 15, Narrator on Isabella awaiting approval of her engagement to James

She was "...most anxiously zealous on the subject..."[7]
Persuasion, Chapter 2, Narrator on Lady Russell's concerns for the Elliot debt

"A thousand alarming presentiments of evil …
must oppress her heart with sadness…"[6]
Northanger Abbey, Chapter 2, Narrator on Mrs. Morland when Catherine
left for Bath

A jittery person

"… one so tremblingly alive to every alarm…"[10]
Catherine, Narrator on Mrs. Percival

He's too timid for his own good

He is "…too diffident to be so agreable as he
might be."[2]
Jane Austen in a letter to Cassandra, Monday, October 11, 1813, about
Mr. John Plumptre[2]

She was terrified

"…her fears had never been so strongly, or
indeed so reasonably, excited."[10]
Catherine, Narrator on Mrs. Percival witnessing Edward Stanley's
attentions to Catherine

Scare him half to death

"…subject him to an alarm which might
seriously affect his health and spirits."[3]
Lady Susan, Chapter 8, Mrs. Vernon to Lady De Courcy about Sir
Reginald's concerns for Mr. De Courcy

She felt hopeless

She "…sat in mournful thought of any
continuance."[1]
Emma, Chapter 1, Narrator – Emma missing Miss Taylor.

He constantly worried about others

"…there was no rest for his benevolent
nerves…"[1]
Emma, Chapter 2, Narrator on Mr. Woodhouse

She was stuck

"… she despaired of effecting her escape…"[10]
Henry and Eliza, Narrator on Eliza escaping the duchess' dungeon

She thinks it's a bad idea

"… she does not at all seem to relish the proposal." [4]
Lesley Castle, Charlotte to Margaret on Eloisa not wanting to marry Mr. Cleveland

To worry people

To "…be the occasion of so much vexation…"[3]
Lady Susan, Chapter 13, Lady De Courcy to Mrs. Vernon

Don't worry about me

"Do not torment yourself with fears on my account…"[3]
Lady Susan, Chapter 33, Lady Susan Vernon to Mrs. Johnson

He always worried about his health

He had "…been a valetudinarian all his life …"[1]
Emma, Chapter 1, Narrator on Mr. Woodhouse

It's scary

"… one's fears cannot but preponderate…"[2]
Jane Austen in a letter to Cassandra, Tuesday, January 10, 1809, about the health of Cassandra's godmother

I don't worry about that

"I have my alarms, but they are quite in a different quarter…"[5]
Mansfield Park, Chapter 22, Mrs. Grant to Mary Crawford about etiquette

It frightened her

It "… was a great increase of … trepidation…"[5]
Mansfield Park, Chapter 23, Narrator on Fanny fear of being seen by Henry Crawford

She dreaded it

"The assurance ... coming upon her like a blow ... was felt with resentment and mortification."[5]
Mansfield Park, Chapter 23, Narrator on Mary Crawford thinking about Edmund entering the clergy

Her concerns

"...anxious considerations, enough to sober her spirits..."[5]
Mansfield Park, Chapter 26, Narrator on Fanny considering how to wear William's gift to the ball

She was scared

"...she sat in trembling wretchedness..."[5]
Mansfield Park, Chapter 32, Narrator on Fanny listening to Sir Thomas' lecture

She "...worked herself into a state of real distress."[6]
Northanger Abbey, Chapter 15, Narrator on Isabella awaiting approval of her engagement to James

"...she was left to the tremors of a most palpitating heart..."[5]
Mansfield Park, Chapter 18, Narrator on Fanny being pressured to stand in for Mrs. Grant's part in the play

She "...was in a good deal of agitation."[5]
Mansfield Park, Chapter 20, Narrator on Maria waiting for Henry Crawford to declare his love

She heard something scary

"... a sound... struck on her affrighted ear."[6]
Northanger Abbey, Chapter 21, Narrator on Catherine's first night at Northanger Abbey

She tried to feel better

She "... sought some suspension of agony..."[6]
Northanger Abbey, Chapter 21, Narrator on Catherine's first night at Northanger Abbey

She was too scared to do it

It "... was an undertaking to frighten away all her powers of performance..."[6]
Northanger Abbey, Chapter 29, Narrator on Catherine writing to Eleanor

He doubted

"He had never indulged much hope..."[7]
Persuasion, Chapter 1, Narrator on Sir Walter's thoughts on Anne

It rattled him

It "... deprived his manners of their usual composure..."[7]
Persuasion, Chapter 9, Narrator on Wentworth's finding himself alone with Anne

Emotionally shaken

"...with most disordered feelings."[7]
Persuasion, Chapter 9, Narrator on Anne being assisted by Wentworth

Uneasiness

"...distressed state of spirits..."[7]
Persuasion, Chapter 13, Narrator on Mr. & Mrs. Musgrove

Carefully

In a "... peculiarly judicious manner..."[6]
Northanger Abbey, Chapter 9, Narrator on John Thorpe holding the reins

She quietly dreaded it

"She persisted in a very determined, though very silent disinclination..."[7]
Persuasion, Chapter 14, Narrator on Anne going to Bath

She dreaded the next hour

"...it chiefly wore the prospect of an hour of agitation."[7]
Persuasion, Chapter 20, Narrator on Anne sitting through the concert

Don't even think that

"... do not foretell vexation from that quarter."[1]
Emma, Chapter 5, Mrs. Weston to Mr. Knightley about the troubles with Frank

She allowed herself to doubt

"...her heart prophesized some mischance to damp the perfection of her felicity."[7]
Persuasion, Chapter 23, Narrator on Anne's fear of Wentworth not attending the party

"Another momentary vexation occurred."[7]
Persuasion, Chapter 23, Narrator on Anne's fear of Wentworth not attending the party

What a horrible thought!

"That is as formidable an image as you could present..."[1]
Emma, Chapter 10, Emma to Harriet about ending up like Miss Bates

He was scared stupid

He "... was silent from consternation..."[1]
Emma, Chapter 15, Narrator on Mr. Woodhouse and the weather

I promise you have nothing to be afraid of

You should be "...convinced by my full and solemn assurance that your fears have been most idly created..."[3]
Lady Susan, Chapter 14, Mr. De Courcy to Sir Reginald

We might lose

"...the honour of victory is doubtful."[3]
Lady Susan, Chapter 25, Lady Susan to Mrs. Johnson

Worry

"... all the pain of apprehension..."[1]
Emma, Chapter 11, Narrator on Emma waiting for John Knightley to get angry with Mr. Woodhouse

His troubled thoughts

"... the inquietude of his mind..."[6]
Northanger Abbey, Chapter 20, Narrator on Captain Tilney's reason for rising late

She was too freaked out to sleep

"With ... feelings in every way so agitated, repose must be absolutely impossible."[6]
Northanger Abbey, Chapter 21, Narrator on Catherine's first night at Northanger Abbey

He's been stressed out

He has"... met with much to disquiet and mortify him..."[7]
Persuasion, Chapter 9, Narrator on Charles Hayter's reaction to Henrietta's behavior

She gets hysterical

She has "...nerves susceptible to the highest extreme of tenderness..."[7]
Persuasion, Chapter 14, Narrator on Louisa's recovery

She was getting nervous

"... the perturbation of... [her] ... feelings was every moment increasing."[8]
Pride and Prejudice, Chapter 44, Narrator on Elizabeth meeting Georgiana Darcy

Worried about what will happen next

"... in general lamentations over the dreadful sequel of this event..."[8]
Pride and Prejudice, Chapter 47, Narrator on Elizabeth & Jane considering the aftermath of Lydia's elopement

She was worried but optimistic

"Anxiety and hope now oppressed her in equal degrees, and left her no moment of tranquility..."[9]

Sense and Sensibility, Volume the Third, Chapter 7, Narrator on Elinor and Marianne's improvement

She calmed his nerves

She "... tranquillized this excess of apprehension..."[1]

Emma, Chapter 13, Narrator on Emma and Mr. Woodhouse's fears about Harriet's cold

To distract her from worry

"... to dissipate some of the distress it occasioned..."[1]

Emma, Chapter 22, Narrator on Harriet visiting the Martins to take her mind off of Mr. Elton

If it's not one problem, it's another

"... the removal of one solicitude generally makes way for another..."[1]

Emma, Chapter 30, Narrator on Mr. Knightley's indifference to the ball

Be careful

"... endeavor ... to secure yourself from so great a danger."[10]

Jack and Alice, Chapter 2, Lady Williams to Alice about falling for Charles Adams

We need to be more careful

"...our affairs... require a delicacy and cautiousness of conduct to which we have hitherto been too little attentive."[3]

Lady Susan, Chapter 30, Lady Susan Vernon to Mr. De Courcy

It could have been worse

"...though the inconvenience has not been nothing, I should have feared still more."[2]
Jane Austen in a letter to Cassandra, Thursday, January 8, 1807, about Jenny being delayed by illness

He hated being late

"...anything like a breach of punctuality was a great offense..."[2]
Jane Austen in a letter to Cassandra, Tuesday, October 26, 1813, about Mr. Moore & the tardy coachman

It was real bad

It "... was an evil which nothing could counterbalance."[6]
Northanger Abbey, Chapter 17, Narrator on Catherine's separation from the Tilneys

Arguments/Disagreements & *Agreements*

Arguing

I'm tired of arguing about this

"We think so very differently on this point ... that there can be no use in canvassing it."[1]

Emma, Chapter 8, Emma to Mr. Knightley about Harriet's expectations of marriage

You're wrong

"Nonsense, errant nonsense, as ever was talked!"[1]

Emma, Chapter 8, Mr. Knightley to Emma about Harriet's expectations of marriage

"It grieves me to say how greatly you were mistaken." [3]

Lady Susan, Chapter 2, Lady Susan Vernon to Mrs. Johnson.

Annoying him

"... provoking him to a rational remonstrance or sharp retort..."[1]

Emma, Chapter 11, Narrator on Mr. Woodhouse's peculiarities on John Knightley

Hanging out without fighting

The "... visit ... might be hoped to pass away in unsullied cordiality."[1]

Emma, Chapter 11, Narrator on the Knightleys' visit

You think you're always right

"To be sure – our discordancies must always arise from my being in the wrong."[1]

Emma, Chapter 12, Emma to Mr. Knightley about their earlier argument over Harriet

Just think about it

"… a silent rumination might suffice…"[1]

Emma, Chapter 12, Narrator on Mr. Woodhouse being upset that the Knightleys went to Southend

Don't bother me

I want "… to be no further incommoded by any troublesome topic…"[1]

Emma, Chapter 19, Narrator on Emma & Harriet's visit to Miss Bates

She denied it

"… the accusation had been eagerly refuted…"[1]

Emma, Chapter 20, Narrator on Emma denying Mr. Knightley's reason Emma didn't like Jane

No way! I don't believe you

"No, I have never had such an idea, and I cannot adopt it now."[1]

Emma, Chapter 26, Emma to Mrs. Weston about Mr. Knightley being in love with Jane

They argued and argued

"They combated the point some time longer in the same way…"[1]

Emma, Chapter 26, Narrator on Emma & Mrs. Weston discussing Mr. Knightley being in love with Jane

They defended him

"They vindicated him against the base aspersion."[1]

Emma, Chapter 34, Narrator on Emma & Mrs. Weston defending Frank's handwriting against Mr. Knightley

I disagree

"... you will find me a formidable antagonist on that point."[1]

Emma, Chapter 36, Mrs. Elton to Mr. Weston, arguing against the delicate nature of women

That's a bunch of bull

"... what a heap of absurdities it is!"[1]

Emma, Chapter 41, Frank to Mr. Weston about the truth in dreams

She wasn't very welcoming

"There was a disagreeable coldness and forbidding reserve in her reception of me..."[10]

Love and Friendship, Letter 7th, Laura to Marianne about meeting Augusta

She is argumentative

Her "...temper could never bear opposition well..."[3]

Lady Susan, Chapter 15, Mrs. Vernon to Lady De Courcy

Of all the things to fight about

"It seems the oddest kind of quarrel in the World..."[2]

Jane Austen in a letter to Cassandra, Thursday, May 21, 1801, about a feud between her aunt & Miss Bond

He disagreed

He "... could not give so instantaneous and unqualified a consent."[5]

Mansfield Park, Chapter 1, Narrator on Sir Thomas' thoughts about taking on Fanny

She didn't like what she saw

"The result of her observations was not agreeable."[6]
Northanger Abbey, Chapter 19, Narrator on Catherine watching Isabella's behavior

They started to disagree

"... on this subject, there began now to be some danger of dissimilarity..."[5]
Mansfield Park, Chapter 7, Narrator on Edmund & Fanny discussing Mary Crawford

They disagreed

They were "... unyielding to his representation..."[5]
Mansfield Park, Chapter 13, Narrator on Maria's & Julia's reaction to Edmund's protests of the play

To yell at them

"... to have them roused... by the remonstrance..."[5]
Mansfield Park, Chapter 14, Narrator on Edmund's reaction to the *Lovers' Vows* script

She pleaded

She "... persevered, and argued the case with so much affectionate earnestness..."[5]
Mansfield Park, Chapter 26, Narrator on Mary Crawford offering a gold necklace to Fanny

She snapped back at her

"... this persuasion did not incline her to a very gracious reply..."[6]
Northanger Abbey, Chapter 8, Narrator on Catherine's response to John Thorpe's request for a dance

She wouldn't cave to their demands

She "... was distressed, but not subdued."[6]

Northanger Abbey, Chapter 13, Narrator on Catherine refusing the Clifton scheme

Couldn't change her mind

"... never succeeded in any point she wanted to carry, against previous inclination."[7]

Persuasion, Chapter 2, Narrator on Elizabeth and Lady Russell

I don't like it

"...I have ... strong grounds of objection to it."[7]

Persuasion, Chapter 3, Sir Walter to Mr. Shepherd referring to the Navy

Why bring that up, after all this time?

"How absurd to be resuming the agitation which such an interval had banished into distance and indistinctness!"[7]

Persuasion, Chapter 7, Anne remonstrating herself

You are making a big deal for nothing

"You are over scrupulous surely."[8]

Pride and Prejudice, Chapter 1, Mr. Bennet to Mrs. Bennet on his need to visit Bingley first

Stop teasing me

"You take delight in vexing me. You have no compassion on my poor nerves."[8]

Pride and Prejudice, Chapter 1, Mrs. Bennet to Mr. Bennet

She would not dignify it with a response

She "...deigned not to make any reply..."[8]

Pride and Prejudice, Chapter 2, Narrator on Mrs. Bennet's response to Mr. Bennet's teasing

Don't put words in my mouth

"You expect me to account for opinions which you chuse to call mine, but which I have never acknowledged."[8]

Pride and Prejudice, Chapter 10, Mr. Darcy to Elizabeth

That's a stupid request

You "... asked it without offering one argument in favour of its propriety."[8]

Pride and Prejudice, Chapter 10, Mr. Darcy to Elizabeth

He ignored her advice

He "... listened to her with the determined air of following his own inclination..."[8]

Pride and Prejudice, Chapter 18, Narrator Mr. Collins introducing himself to Mr. Darcy

Why bring that up again

"... it is not genteel to rip up old grievances."[2]

Jane Austen in a letter to Cassandra, Tuesday, January 24, 1809, complaining about the weather

I'm going to do what I think is right

"You must therefore allow me to follow the dictates of my conscience on this occasion..."[8]

Pride and Prejudice, Chapter 18, Mr. Collins to Elizabeth on her objection to his introducing himself to Mr. Darcy

I'm not listening to you

You will have to "Pardon me for neglecting to profit by your advice..."[8]

Pride and Prejudice, Chapter 18, Mr. Collins to Elizabeth on her objection to his introducing himself to Mr. Darcy

I know better than you do

"...I consider myself more fitted by education and habitual study to decide on what is right..."[8]
Pride and Prejudice, Chapter 18, Mr. Collins to Elizabeth on her objection to his introducing himself to Mr. Darcy

She argued her point

"She represented... as forcibly as possible what she felt on the subject..."[8]
Pride and Prejudice, Chapter 21, Narrator on Elizabeth's discussion with Jane over Caroline Bingley's letter

To be unimpressive

"... to form that ground-work of disapprobation..."[8]
Pride and Prejudice, Chapter 34, Elizabeth to Mr. Darcy explaining her dislike of him

She couldn't be convinced

"... her mind could not acquiesce."[8]
Pride and Prejudice, Chapter 42, Narrator on Elizabeth's reluctance to visit Pemberley

She disagreed

"...so many had been her objections against such a measure..."[9]
Sense and Sensibility, Volume the Second, Chapter 4, Narrator on Elinor and the London trip

I tried to forgive you

"I have passed a wretched night in endeavoring to excuse a conduct which can scarcely be called less than insulting..."[9]
Sense and Sensibility, Volume the Second, Chapter 7, Marianne in a letter to Willoughby

They argued without facts

"...it was all conjectural assertion on both sides..."[9]
Sense and Sensibility, Volume the Second, Chapter 12, Narrator on Mrs. John Dashwood & Lady Middleton

She lashed out

"...her vehemence made reserve impossible..."[9]
Sense and Sensibility, Volume the Third, Chapter 1, Narrator on Marianne, Elinor, and Mrs. Jennings after listening to John Dashwood

She stared him down

"... her eyes ... fixed on him with a look that spoke ... contempt..."[9]
Sense and Sensibility, Volume the Third, Chapter 5, Narrator on Elinor & Robert Ferrars

He better get it right

"If he were deficient there, nothing should make amends for it."[1]
Emma, Chapter 24, Narrator on Frank's treatment of Mrs. Weston

I love putting him in his place

"There is exquisite pleasure in subduing an insolent spirit..."[3]
Lady Susan, Chapter 7, Lady Susan Vernon to Mrs. Johnson

Hurt them

"...excited their anguish..."[3]
Lady Susan, Chapter 34, Mr. De Courcy to Lady Susan

I have a problem with that

"In one particular I could wish it otherwise..."[2]
Jane Austen in a letter to Cassandra, Thursday, September 15, 1796, about arriving so early

You knew it was wrong

"... You had some doubts of the propriety of such a measure yourself."[2]
Jane Austen in a letter to Cassandra, Tuesday, December 18, 1798, about Cassandra writing to Sir Thomas Williams

She'd rather not

She "... was at first very little inclined, or rather totally disinclined..."[2]
Jane Austen in a letter to Cassandra, Tuesday, August 27, 1805, about Louisa Hatton accepting Lady Forbes' offer

To avoid another nagging lecture

"To save herself from useless remonstrance..."[5]
Mansfield Park, Chapter 1, Narrator on Mrs. Price not writing to her family

She grew tired of him

"His presence was beginning to be odious to her..."[5]
Mansfield Park, Chapter 20, Narrator on Maria & Mr. Rushworth

She shot him down

She "... hoped to silence him with such an extremity of reproof..."[5]
Mansfield Park, Chapter 34, Narrator on Fanny's reply to Henry Crawford's comment to Edmund

They were very different

"... there could not be two persons in existence whose characters and manners were less accordant..."[5]
Mansfield Park, Chapter 30, Narrator on Fanny & Admiral Crawford

"... there was scarcely a second feeling in common between them..."[5]
Mansfield Park, Chapter 37, Narrator on Edmund & Mary Crawford

Getting Along & Agreeing

They're getting along well

"He had been ... with her ... most companionably..."[1]
Emma, Chapter 24, Narrator on Frank & Mrs. Weston

I agree with you

"Your reasonings carry my judgment along with them entirely."[1]
Emma, Chapter 26, Frank to Emma about Mr. Dixon giving Jane the pianoforte

"I am quite of your opinion."[7]
Persuasion, Chapter 8, Mrs. Musgrove agreeing with Mrs. Croft

You can't argue with that
"...what could be offered but general acquiescence?"[7]
Persuasion, Chapter 12, Narrator on Anne listening to Henrietta

We aim to please

"To do what would be most generally pleasing must be our object..."[1]
Emma, Chapter 29, Mrs. Weston on choosing accommodations for the ball

She agreed

"... she gave a very proper compliance."[1]
Emma, Chapter 26, Narrator on Emma playing the piano at the Coles' party

She "... did not evince the least disapprobation."[5]
Mansfield Park, Chapter 13, Narrator on Lady Bertram's reaction to the suggestion of a play

She "...assented most feelingly to the remark..."[9]
Sense and Sensibility, Volume the Third, Chapter 11, Narrator on Marianne's response to Elinor's assessment of Willoughby's problems

I promise

"If I meet with no insuperable difficulties, therefore, consider that point as settled."[1]
Emma, Chapter 34, Mrs. Elton to Jane about fetching Jane's letters for her

She almost said it, but didn't

"... it was at her tongue's end – but she abstained."[1]
Emma, Chapter 34, Narrator on Emma almost asking Jane about a letter from Ireland

I'm sure I'll like him

"... I assure you ... I have very little doubt that my opinion will be decidedly in his favor."[1]
Emma, Chapter 36, Mrs. Elton to Mr. Weston about Frank

I'm sorry

"I believe there will be need of even all your goodness to allow for some parts of my past conduct."[1]
Emma, Chapter 50, Frank in a letter to Mrs. Weston

Her approval

Her "... gay acquiescence..."[6]
Northanger Abbey, Chapter 13, Narrator on Catherine's thoughts on the Clifton scheme

Everyone agreed

"There was not a dissentient voice on the subject..."[1]
Emma, Chapter 2, Narrator on Frank's obligation to visit

"...every one concerned ... was forward in expressing their ready concurrence..."[5]
Mansfield Park, Chapter 6, Narrator on the plans to see Sotherton

"...our sentiments coincided in every particular..."[8]
Pride and Prejudice, Chapter 7, Mr. Bennet to Mrs. Bennet on the character of Catherine and Lydia

He agreed to it

"...his most hearty concurrence was conveyed..."[5]
Mansfield Park, Chapter 4, Narrator on Sir Thomas' approval of Maria's match with Mr. Rushworth

He "... was eager to assure her ... of his acquiescence..."[5]
Mansfield Park, Chapter 6, Narrator on Mr Rushworth's agreeing with Lady Bertram about his shrubberies

He "... was too polite to make further opposition."[6]
Northanger Abbey, Chapter 22, Narrator on General Tilney allowing Miss Tilney's path

His "... approbation secured..."[6]
Northanger Abbey, Chapter 13, Narrator on John Thorpe's approval of the Clifton scheme

You like my idea

"... you are both all compliance with my scheme..."[2]
Jane Austen in a letter to Cassandra, Thursday, June 6, 1811, about Miss Sharp travelling with Cassandra & Martha

She was cool with it

She "...gave a most good-humoured acquiescence."[7]
Persuasion, Chapter 19, Narrator on Mrs. Smith excusing Anne's missed visit

It was a good idea

"Everyone capable of thinking felt the advantage of the idea..."[7]
Persuasion, Chapter 12, Narrator on Benwick seeking a surgeon for Louisa

"...it would be a very eligible ... plan..."[2]
Jane Austen in a letter to Cassandra, Thursday, September 15, 1796, about Edward taking the name Claringbould

"... it would be no more than common prudence..."[1]
Emma, Chapter 13, Emma to Mr. Elton about staying home from the Westons' party

"It appears to me the most desirable arrangement in the world."[1]
Emma, Chapter 19, Emma to Miss Bates about Jane coming home for her health

"... it must be scrupulousness run mad, that could see anything to censure in a plan like theirs..."[5]
Mansfield Park, Chapter 13, Narrator on Thomas', Maria's & Julia's opinion of doing a play

I try not to judge

"I would wish not to be too hasty in censuring any one."[8]
Pride and Prejudice, Chapter 4, Jane to Elizabeth

Everybody knows that

"It is a truth universally acknowledged..."[8]
Pride and Prejudice, Chapter 1, Narrator with one of the most famous opening lines in literary history

Everyone agrees with that

"... there cannot be two opinions on that point."[8]
Pride and Prejudice, Chapter 5, Charlotte recalling the words of Mr. Bingley

Obvious to her

"... so decided to her eye..."[5]
Mansfield Park, Chapter 18, Narrator on Fanny's notice of Maria avoiding Mr. Rushworth

Who wouldn't go for that?

"... considering the inducement... we cannot wonder at his compliance..."[8]
Pride and Prejudice, Chapter 6, Sir William to Elizabeth on Mr. Darcy's willingness to dance with her

Hey, whatever you say

"Allowing the case, however, to stand according to your representation..."[8]
Pride and Prejudice, Chapter 10, Mr. Darcy to Elizabeth

Whatever you like

"I would by no means suspend any pleasure of yours..."[8]
Pride and Prejudice, Chapter 18, Mr. Darcy to Elizabeth

They happily agreed

"...their consent... was bestowed with a most joyful alacrity."[8]
Pride and Prejudice, Chapter 22, Narrator on the Charlotte's parents agreeing to the marriage to Mr. Collins

I'll get her opinion first

"...you may depend upon my not taking so material a step without her...concurrence."[8]
Pride and Prejudice, Chapter 22, Mr. Collins to Mr. Bennet on revisiting Longbourne

I think you will come to like her

"...your kind impressions in her favour will, I am sure, be heightened."[3]
Lady Susan, Chapter 18, Mrs. Vernon to Lady De Courcy

They're not so bad

"...I cannot utterly abhor them..."[2]

Jane Austen in a letter to Cassandra, Thursday, May 21, 1801, about Mrs. & Miss Holder

I don't mind

"It would not be so great an objection to me..."[2]

Jane Austen in a letter to Anna Austen, Thursday, August 18, 1814, about some objections to Anna's novel

Humor us

"We bespeak your indulgence..."[5]

Mansfield Park, Chapter 19, Mr. Yates to Sir Thomas on watching a rehearsal

They stayed out of it

"...they were not refined enough to make any parading stipulation..."[6]

Northanger Abbey, Chapter 30, Narrator on the Morlands not demanding that General Tilney embrace the engagement

Meetings & Greetings

Meetings

I'd like to get to know them

"It would give me particular pleasure to have an opportunity of improving my acquaintance with..."[2] them.

Jane Austen in a letter to Cassandra, Saturday, November 17, 1798, quoting a letter Mrs. Lefroy received about the Austens

We want to get to know her better

"With ... pleasure we anticipate an intimacy with her..."[2]

Jane Austen in a letter to Cassandra, Tuesday, December 28, 1808, about Mr. Digweed's bailiff & his wife

She wants to get to know them better

She "... means to cultivate the acquaintance..."[2]

Jane Austen in a letter to Cassandra, Thursday, April 25, 1811, about Eliza & the D'Entraigues

She wanted to get to know him better

"They ... parted, on the lady's side at least, with a strong inclination for continuing the acquaintance."[6]

Northanger Abbey, Chapter 3, Narrator on Catherine & Mr. Tilney

A good place to meet girls

A place "...so favourable for the discovery of female excellence and the completion of female intimacy..."[6]

Northanger Abbey, Chapter 9, Narrator on the Pump-room

Being approached by a good person

"...being spontaneously solicited by some most unexceptionable applicant..."[7]
Persuasion, Chapter 2, Narrator on Sir Walter meeting poeple

He was warmly welcomed

"There was so much of friendliness, and of flattery, and of everything most bewitching in his reception there..."[7]
Persuasion, Chapter 9, Narrator on Wentworth at Uppercross

Desperate stalking

"...such assiduous endeavors to meet..."[7]
Persuasion, Chapter 15, Narrator on Mr. Elliot's visits to Camden Place

He was pleased to meet her

"... with the most perfect alacrity he welcomed the relationship..."[7]
Persuasion, Chapter 15, Narrator on Mr. Elliot being introduced to Anne

He made a good first impression

"His manners were an immediate recommendation..."[7]
Persuasion, Chapter 16, Narrator on Mr. Elliot & Lady Russell

We try too hard to impress them

"I certainly do think there has been far too much trouble taken to procure the acquaintance."[7]
Persuasion, Chapter 16, Anne on the Dalrymples

I hate those kinds of get-togethers

"... there is something insufferably tedious in the usual process of such a meeting."[8]
Pride and Prejudice, Chapter 11, Caroline Bingley to Mr. Darcy & Mr. Bingley on the Netherfield ball

He was eager to get to know them

"The introduction was followed up on his side by a happy readiness of conversation..."[8]

Pride and Prejudice, Chapter 15, Narrator on Mr. Wickham meeting the Misses Bennet

It was unlikely that they should run into each other

"She felt all the perverseness of the mischance that should bring him where no one else was brought..."[8]

Pride and Prejudice, Chapter 33, Narrator on Elizabeth running into Mr. Darcy during her walks at Rosings Park

I don't know him that well

"I have not had so many opportunities of estimating the minuter propensities of his mind..."[9]

Sense and Sensibility, Volume the First, Chapter 4, Marianne to Elinor on Edward Ferrars

He put off a good first impression

He was "...instantly the theme of general admiration..."[9]

Sense and Sensibility, Volume the First, Chapter 9, Narrator on Willoughby

Breaking the ice

"...opening the first trenches of an acquaintance..."[3]

Sanditon, Chapter 10, Narrator on Diana Parker's efforts for Mrs. Griffiths

She wanted to check him out

She "... was not sorry to have such an opportunity of survey..."[1]

Emma, Chapter 4, Narrator on Emma seeing Robert Martin

She "... soon made her quick eye acquainted with..."[1] him.

Emma, Chapter 4, Narrator on Emma seeing Robert Martin

They met under bad circumstances

"... their acquaintance had begun in dilapidations..."[5]

Mansfield Park, Chapter 6, Narrator on Mrs. Norris & Dr. Grant

---

She says 'Hello'

"She desires her best love to you and kind remembrance..."[2]

Jane Austen in a letter to Cassandra, Thursday, October 21, 1813, about Harriot Moore[2]

She welcomed him

She "... received him with the simplest professions of unaffected benevolence..."[6]

Northanger Abbey, Chapter 30, Narrator on Mrs. Morland greeting Mr. Tilney

They were glad to see her

"... she was welcomed by her two friends with many professions of pleasure..."[8]

Pride and Prejudice, Chapter 11, Narrator on Miss Bingley & Mrs. Hurst welcoming Jane

She wanted me to tell you 'Hi'

"... she desired to be kindly remembered to you..."[2]

Jane Austen in a letter to Cassandra, Friday, January 29, 1813, about Miss Benn

Friendship &
Sympathy/Pity

Friendship

They talked freely

They "… tasted the sweets of friendship in an unreserved conversation…"[6]

Northanger Abbey, Chapter 5, Narrator on Isabella's conversations with Catherine

Your pals will help you get over heartache

"Friendship is certainly the finest balm for the pangs of disappointed love."[6]

Northanger Abbey, Chapter 4, Narrator on Catherine with the Miss Thorpes

They quickly became close

"… they passed so rapidly through every gradation of increasing tenderness…"[6]

Northanger Abbey, Chapter 5, Narrator on Catherine & Isabella

Their closeness

"… their precious intercourse of friendship and confidence…"[1]

Emma, Chapter 48, Narrator on Emma's wishes for her future with Mr. Knightley

I'm a loyal friend

"When once my affections are placed, it is not in the power of any thing to change them."[6]

Northanger Abbey, Chapter 13, Isabella to Catherine

An old, dear classmate

"… a former school-fellow and intimate…"[6]
Northanger Abbey, Chapter 4, Narrator on Mrs. Thorpe

Befriend a stranger

"… bestow … affection and confidence on one who ought to have been nothing … but the object of distant civility."[7]
Persuasion, Chapter 2, Narrator on Elizabeth and Mrs. Clay

They took good care of her

"every thing that the most zealous affection, the most solicitous care, could do to render her comfortable, was the office of each watchful companion…"[9]
Sense and Sensibility, Volume the Third, Chapter 10, Narrator on the Dashwoods' trip back to Barton

I'm glad they're friends

"… I cannot lament the acquaintance."[1]
Emma, Chapter 5, Mrs. Weston to Mr. Knightley about Emma & Harriet

A friend told me how you have been using me

"…I have received from indisputable authority such a history of you as must bring the most mortifying conviction of the imposition I have been under…"[3]
Lady Susan, Chapter 34, Mr. De Courcy to Lady Susan

I want you to like me

"…to be sunk… in your esteem is a humiliation to which I know not how to submit."[3]
Lady Susan, Chapter 35, Lady Susan to Mr. De Courcy

He was just messing with her

"He was … but at treacherous play with her."[5]
Mansfield Park, Chapter 14, Narrator on Henry Crawford's appeal to cast Julia as Amelia

She saw only the good

"… her conscience must have restrained her from venturing at disapprobation."[5]
Mansfield Park, Chapter 18, Narrator on Fanny critiquing Edmund's rehearsal with Mary Crawford

She thought it was a perfect gift

She "…was exceedingly pleased with an acquisition so very apropos."[5]
Mansfield Park, Chapter 26, Narrator on Fanny about Mary Crawford's gift of the gold necklace

I just want to make you happy

"… I have no pleasure in the world superior to that of contributing to yours. No, I can safely say, I have no pleasure so complete, so unalloyed. It is without drawback."[5]
Mansfield Park, Chapter 27, Edmund to Fanny upon giving her the gold chain

Sympathy/Pity

Too bad for her

"… her situation is so calculated to affect one!"[1]
Emma, Chapter 33, Mrs. Elton to Emma about Jane

Things look bad for her

"Whatever advantages she may have enjoyed … are so palpably at an end!"[1]
Emma, Chapter 33, Mrs. Elton to Emma about Jane

You should feel bad for her

"Her situation should secure your compassion."[1]
Emma, Chapter 43, Mr. Knightley to Emma about Miss Bates

She told a sad story

"At this melancholy recital the fair eyes ... were suffused in tears."[10]
Jack and Alice, Chapter 6, Narrator on Lady Williams' reaction to Lucy's story

This'll make you sad

"... your sensibility will be most severely tried."[10]
Love and Friendship, Letter 14th, Laura to Marianne about Sophia's death

We sympathized

"... we joined in heartfelt lamentations..."[4]
Lesley Castle, Charlotte to Margaret on wasting the food

I sympathized

"...I felt for her exceedingly."[3]
Lady Susan, Chapter 20, Mrs. Vernon to Lady De Courcy

It makes me sad

"My tears flow ... at the melancholy idea."[2]
Jane Austen in a letter to Cassandra, Thursday January 14, 1796, about Tom Lefroy getting married

We're sorry for your loss

"... You must accept ... our sincere Condolance on the melancholy Event..."[2]
Jane Austen in a letter to Philadelphia Walter, Sunday, April 8, 1798, about the death of his father

He's had it tough

His "... history is a melancholy one."[2]
Jane Austen in a letter to Cassandra, Wednesday, June 19, 1799, about John Lyford

I feel sorry for him

"One is really obliged to engage in Pity again on his account..."[2]
Jane Austen in a letter to Martha Lloyd, Tuesday, February 16, 1813, about John Harwood's financial problems

Feeling sorry for her friend

"... deeply commiserating the state of her poor friend..."[6]
Northanger Abbey, Chapter 24, Narrator on Catherine after Eleanor was caught in the gallery

They were empathetic

They were "... as open as they were sincere, in their exclamations of pity and horror."[7]
Persuasion, Chapter 8, Narrator on the Miss Musgroves' reaction to Wentworth's stories

She is sensitive

She has "... a heart to sympathize in any of the sufferings it occasioned..."[7]
Persuasion, Chapter 9, Narrator on Henrietta

Just as bad off

"... scarcely less an object of pity!"[9]
Sense and Sensibility, Volume the Third, Chapter 7, Narrator on Col. Brandon compared to Mrs. Dashwood

He sympathized

"... he joined most heartily in the general regret on so unfortunate an event..."[9]
Sense and Sensibility, Volume the First, Chapter 13, Narrator on Sir John and the Whitwell excursion

I helped

"I have, of course, tendered my services..."[2]
Jane Austen in a letter to Cassandra, Thursday, June 16, 1808, about helping with the children at Godmersham

She sympathized

She "... spoke her concern in an exclamation of tender concern..."[9]
Sense and Sensibility, Volume the Second, Chapter 9, Narrator on Elinor listening to Col. Brandon's story

She "... sat sighing and moralizing ... with a commiseration and good sense..."[1]
Emma, Chapter 45, Narrator Mrs. Weston after Mrs. Churchill's death

Wanting to help her

"... desirous to share in all her fatigues..."[9]
Sense and Sensibility, Volume the Third, Chapter 5, Narrator on Mrs. Jennings when Marianne was sick

She's on our minds

She "... is the heroine of our thoughts..."[2]
Jane Austen in a letter to Cassandra, Monday, October 24, 1808, about Lady Bridges

I just want to feel important

"... it would be delightful to feel myself of consequence to anybody."[5]
Mansfield Park, Chapter 3, Fanny to Edmund on the idea of moving in with Mrs. Norris

I will try to sympathize with him

"I shall prepare my most plaintive airs against his return..."[5]
Mansfield Park, Chapter 6, Mary Crawford to Edmund about Thomas' horse losing the race

She is in a pickle

"She is awkwardly circumstanced."[5]
Mansfield Park, Chapter 7, Edmund to Fanny about Mary Crawford

Accomodations

She has a bad view from her room

"...the prospect from her window is not very instructive..."[3]

Lady Susan, Chapter 17, Mrs. Vernon to Lady De Courcy

I won't mind moving (homes)

"I get more & more reconciled to the idea of our removal."[2]

Jane Austen in a letter to Cassandra, Saturday, January 3, 1801, about the move to Bath

Way too small

"... quite monstrously little..."[2]

Jane Austen in a letter to Cassandra, Thursday, May 21, 1801, about the houses in New King Street

They gave us big bedrooms

"... we were most commodiously disposed of."[2]

Jane Austen in a letter to Cassandra, Wednesday, September 15, 1813, about their rooms at Henrietta St.

Nice digs

"... a house commodious and well fitted up..."[5]

Mansfield Park, Chapter 4, Narrator on Mary Crawford's opinion of Mrs. Grant's house

They were fancy rooms

"... every thing that money and taste could do, to give comfort and elegance to apartments, had been bestowed on these..."[6]

Northanger Abbey, Chapter 23, Narrator on Catherine's tour of the abbey

It was a big room

"The room ... was of a commodious, well-proportioned size..."[6]
Northanger Abbey, Chapter 26, Narrator on Mr. Tilney's parsonage

Convincing & Deciding

Convincing

She gave in

"... it was impossible for her ... not to accede to it more readily than her own judgment authorized."[5]
Mansfield Park, Chapter 36, Narrator on Fanny's inability to refuse Mary Crawford

He "... urged her ... with an earnestness which she could not resist..."[5]
Mansfield Park, Chapter 9, Narrator on Edmund convincing Fanny to rest

"The lady could not but yield to such joint entreaties..."[7]
Persuasion, Chapter 16, Narrator on Mrs. Clay deciding to stay in Bath

They convinced him

He "... was induced by the entreaties of both..."[1]
Emma, Chapter 8, Narrator on Emma & Mr. Knightley convincing Mr. Woodhouse to take a walk

They convinced her

"... she had no scruples which could stand many minutes against the earnest pressing of both the others."[1]
Emma, Chapter 6, Narrator on Harriet agreeing to sit for a portrait

He came to talk me out of it

"...he came to expostulate with me..."[3]
Lady Susan, Chapter 24, Mrs. Vernon to Lady De Courcy

Make him believe her

"Make him really confide in her sincerity." 3
Lady Susan, Chapter 3, Mrs. Vernon to Lady De Courcy

Trying to convince her

"... saying everything she could think of to
obviate the scruples..."5
Mansfield Park, Chapter 26, Narrator on Mary Crawford offering a gold
necklace to Fanny

She's easily swayed

"Her opinion varying with every fresh
conjecture..."9
Sense and Sensibility, Volume the First, Chapter 14, Narrator on Mrs.
Jennings' thoughts on Col. Brandon's departure

She convinced her

"Her ... earnest, though gentle persuasion ...
soon softened her to compliance..."9
Sense and Sensibility, Volume the Second, Chapter 8, Narrator on Elinor
convincing Marianne to sleep

They talked me out of it

"... they dissuaded me from so rash a step..."2
Jane Austen in a letter to Cassandra, Sunday, September 18, 1796,
about going with Frank the next day

They seemed obvious

"... they were supported by such appearances as
made their dismissal impossible."6
Northanger Abbey, Chapter 23, Narrator on Catherine's surmises
concerning General & Mrs. Tilney

He didn't take no for an answer

"He was armed against the highest pitch of
distain or aversion." 3
Sanditon, Chapter 8, Narrator on Sir Edward's attempted seduction of
Clara

It was excusable

"It had a high claim to forbearance."[1]
Emma, Chapter 11, Narrator on John Knighley preferring to stay at home

I'm not interested

I am "… determined against its exciting any present curiosity…"[1]
Emma, Chapter 30, Narrator on Mr. Knightley's indifference to the ball

Trust me

"I know enough … to speak decidedly on that point."[1]
Emma, Chapter 33, Mrs. Elton to Emma about Jane musical talent

She'll have a chance to impress me

"She will have occasion for all those attractive powers, for which she is celebrated, to gain any share of my regard." [3]
Lady Susan, Chapter 3, Mrs. Vernon to Lady De Courcy.

She won him over

"…she has entirely effaced all his former ill-opinion…" [3]
Lady Susan, Chapter 11, Mrs. Vernon to Lady De Courcy

You believed it

"…you had no doubt of its authenticity…" [3]
Lady Susan, Chapter 12, Sir Reginald De Courcy to his son

To make an excuse

"…to assign any cause for her extraordinary conduct…"[3]
Lady Susan, Chapter 16, Lady Susan to Mrs. Johnson

To hate doubters

To "...look with a degree of contempt on the inquisitive and doubtful fancies of that heart which seems always debating on the reasonableness of its emotions."[3]
Lady Susan, Chapter 16, Lady Susan to Mrs. Johnson

They couldn't talk her into staying

"... not all that could be urged to detain her succeeded."[1]
Emma, Chapter 19, Narrator on Emma leaving Miss Bates before hearing Jane's letter

He tried to win me over

"He endeavoured ... to soften my resentment..."[3]
Lady Susan, Chapter 22, Lady Susan to Mrs. Johnson

I tried to appear confident but stern

"If my countenance expressed what I aimed at, it was composed and dignified; and yet, with a degree of pensiveness which might convince him that I was not quite happy."[3]
Lady Susan, Chapter 25, Lady Susan to Mrs. Johnson

Hey, whatever she says

"... I cannot carry my complaisance farther than to believe whatever she asserts on the subject."[2]
Jane Austen in a letter to Cassandra, Monday, November 30, 1800, about Martha growing fat

Can we get on with it?

I am "... urging the execution of the plan ... which ... had since lain dormant."[5]
Mansfield Park, Chapter 8, Narrator on Mrs. Rushworth's desire for the plan to visit Sotherton

I didn't know why

"... I had no reason to give for its necessity."[2]

Jane Austen in a letter to Cassandra, Friday, August 30, 1805, about leaving Goodnestone Farm the next day

It's urgent

It "... is a point of the first expediency..."[2]

Jane Austen in a letter to Cassandra, Friday, August 30, 1805, about the journey to London from Goodnestone Farm

They ain't fooling me

"I shall certainly endeavour to guard myself against their influence."[3]

Lady Susan, Chapter 3, Mrs. Vernon to Lady De Courcy

Forced into it

"...in the hateful predicament of being obliged..."[2]

Jane Austen in a letter to Cassandra, Sunday, November 20, 1808, about letter writing

It doesn't matter what it looks like

"The appearance need not signify."[2]

Jane Austen in a letter to Cassandra, Tuesday, October 12, 1813, about the width of a door

Don't let me get in the way

"... far be it from me to throw any fanciful impediment in the way of a plan..."[5]

Mansfield Park, Chapter 1, Sir Thomas to Lady Bertram & Mrs. Norris about taking on Fanny

Talking it up

"... most zealous in promoting ... by every suggestion and contrivance likely to enhance its desirableness..."[5]

Mansfield Park, Chapter 4, Narrator on Mrs. Norris' promotion of Maria's match with Mr. Rushworth

He had a moment of weakness

He "... had descended from that moral elevation which he had maintained before..."[5]
Mansfield Park, Chapter 17, Narrator on Edmund's decision to be in the play

Don't you dare

"I shall despise you ... most insufferably if you do."[2]
Jane Austen in a letter to Cassandra, Monday, November 30, 1800, about missing the Canterbury Ball

To cave to their whims

"... to sacrifice his own happiness to the caprice of their inclinations."[8]
Pride and Prejudice, Chapter 24, Narrator on Elizabeth's disgust with Mr. Bingley's weakness

He caved

"... he had not cared enough about it to persevere against a few repulses..."[5]
Mansfield Park, Chapter 17, Narrator on Henry Crawford's attempt to smooth things over between Julia & Maria

"He was not ill-inclined to obey..."[6]
Northanger Abbey, Chapter 30, Narrator on Mr. Tilney agreeing not to talk about the past

He stopped bugging her about it

He "... resolved to abstain from all further importunity ... and to show no open interference."[5]
Mansfield Park, Chapter 33, Narrator on Sir Thomas trusting that Henry Crawford would eventually win over Fanny

Hard-headedness

"... a perseverance ... against discouragement."[5]
Mansfield Park, Chapter 33, Sir Thomas to Fanny on Henry Crawford's optimism

He needed encouragement

"... he did not think he could have gone on ... without something more to warm his courage..."[5]
Mansfield Park, Chapter 34, Narrator on Edmund's opinion of Fanny & Henry Crawford

They were forced to behave

They "... were restrained from some excesses of very offensive indulgence and vulgarity."[5]
Mansfield Park, Chapter 40, Narrator on Mrs. Price & Betsy

He had to win her over

"... he must exert himself to subdue so proud a display of resentment..."[5]
Mansfield Park, Chapter 48, Narrator Henry Crawford seducing Maria

Asking Favors

She begged

She "... was very earnest in her application..."[9]
Sense and Sensibility, Volume the Second, Chapter 5, Narrator on Elinor writing to Mrs. Dashwood

She was looking for help

"... she was at that moment in quest of a person to employ on the errand..."[3]
The Watsons, Tom Musgrave to Emma about the note from Elizabeth

She nagged on and on

She was "... indefatigable in her enquiries..."9
Sense and Sensibility, Volume the First, Chapter 3, Narrator on Mrs. Dashwood looking for a place to live

He bugged the heck out of them

"... his entreaties were carried to a point of perseverance beyond civility..."9
Sense and Sensibility, Volume the First, Chapter 6, Narrator on Sir John upon the Dashwood's arrival at Barton

If it's okay with her

"... provided it meet with her approbation."3
Sanditon, Chapter 12, Mr. Parker to Mrs. Parker about Lady Denham helping the Mullinses

She couldn't ask so much of him

"She could not endure the thought! She would not give him such a troublesome office for all the world..."1
Emma, Chapter 6, Narrator on Emma and Mr. Elton's offer to frame Harriet's portrait

Her friend kept bugging her

"The pertinacity of her friend seemed more than she could bear."1
Emma, Chapter 42, Narrator on Mrs. Elton pressing Jane to accept the position she arranged

You are too nice. I can't ask you to do that

"... as I cannot have any doubt of the warmth of your affection, I am far from exacting so heavy a sacrifice." 3
Lady Susan, Chapter 7, Lady Susan Vernon to Mrs. Johnson

A gift with strings attached

A "...Resignation with such Incumbrances."[2]
Jane Austen in a letter to Cassandra, Tuesday, January 8, 1799, about Mrs. Knight giving an estate to Edward

If you don't mind

"... if your Will is not perverse..."[2]
Jane Austen in a letter to Martha Lloyd, Wednesday, November 12, 1800, inviting her to visit

How can you ask such a thing?

"You distress me cruelly by your request..."[2]
Jane Austen in a letter to Martha Lloyd, Wednesday, November 12, 1800, about Jane bringing books with her visit

That's a lot to ask of him

"... that would be to give him trouble without any counterpoise of convenience..."[2]
Jane Austen in a letter to Cassandra, Wednesday, February 11, 1801, about James accompanying Cassandra to London

I don't want to be any trouble

"I shall at any rate be glad not to be obliged to be an incumbrance..."[2]
Jane Austen in a letter to Cassandra, Wednesday, June 15, 1808, about being conveyed by Mr. Trimmer

How dare she even ask it?

"... I wonder at her imprudence in proposing it."[2]
Jane Austen in a letter to Cassandra, Thursday, June 30, 1808, about Martha expecting to hear from Jane

I'd like that

"... it will be a fresh matter of delight to me..."[5]
Mansfield Park, Chapter 4, Mary Crawford to Mrs. Grant on the hopes of matching Henry to Julia

He kept begging

He "... continued his supplication."[5]
Mansfield Park, Chapter 14, Narrator on Henry Crawford's appeal to cast Julia as Amelia

To ask permission of

To "... entreat the sanction of..."[5]
Mansfield Park, Chapter 32, Narrator on Henry Crawford asking Sit Thomas for Fanny's hand

Begging

"... such tender, such flattering supplication..."[6]
Northanger Abbey, Chapter 13, Narrator on Isabella's attempts to convince Catherine of the Clifton scheme

I don't care

"... it is quite a matter of indifference to me."[6]
Northanger Abbey, Chapter 14, Anne Thorpe to Catherine about not going to Clifton

Deciding

I had no choice

"... the necessity of the case will plead my excuse..."[10]
Catherine, Edward Stanley to Catherine on why he came as he did

She considered it

"... she fell into a train of thinking on the subject..."[1]
Emma, Chapter 26, Narrator on Emma watching Mr. Knightley admire Jane's playing

It really matters

It "… would have all the usual weight and efficacy."[1]
Emma, Chapter 4, Narrator on the effect of Mr. Elton's preference on Harriet

I need a good excuse

"… I cannot think of any tolerable pretense…"[1]
Emma, Chapter 10, Emma to Harriet about visiting the vicarage

I'm not even tempted

"I have none of the usual inducements…"[1]
Emma, Chapter 10, Emma to Harriet about marrying

Sounds tempting

"… that would certainly be a most powerful inducement…"[10]
Catherine, Catherine to Edward Stanley on being talked about

My mind is made up

"…I am unalterably fixed on this point…"[3]
Lady Susan, Chapter 19, Lady Susan to Mrs. Johnson

I can't decide what to do

"…at present my thoughts are fluctuating between various schemes."[3]
Lady Susan, Chapter 25, Lady Susan to Mrs. Johnson

I'm going to do things my way

"I am tired of submitting my will to the caprices of others; of resigning my own judgment in deference…"[3]
Lady Susan, Chapter 39, Lady Susan to Mrs. Johnson

She had not made up her mind

"…her own plans were not yet wholly fixed…"[3]
Lady Susan, Conclusion, Narrator to Reader

We decided not to do it

"The … scheme … was by general, and I believe very hearty, consent dissolved."[2]
Jane Austen in a letter to Cassandra, Wednesday, June 15, 1808, about a brewery visit

You can still change your mind

"… your arrangements … may admit od suitable alteration."[2]
Jane Austen in a letter to Cassandra, Sunday, November 20, 1808, about changing plans to accommodate Frank's visit

For obvious reasons

To "… have a motive which can leave nothing to conjecture…"[2]
Jane Austen in a letter to Cassandra, Monday, January 30, 1809, about why Cassandra checks in on the house & garden

I'm pretty sure I'll go

"… I consider my Goings as tolerably fixed."[2]
Jane Austen in a letter to Cassandra, Thursday, April 18, 1811, about a visit to Mrs. Hill in Streatham

He did that on purpose

"There might be design in this, to be sure, on his side…"[2]
Jane Austen in a letter to Cassandra, Sunday, January 24, 1813, about Mr. Papillon neglecting to feed Miss Patience Terry[2]

A whim

"… the consequence of an inclination…"[5]
Mansfield Park, Chapter 7, Narrator on Mary Crawford learning how to ride

She decided

She was "... retired in proud resolve..."[5]
Mansfield Park, Chapter 21, Narrator on Maria's intention to marry Mr. Rushworth

She shouldn't have even considered it

"It ought not to have touched on the confines of her imagination."[5]
Mansfield Park, Chapter 27, Narrator on Fanny's romantic thoughts for Edmund

He made no plans

He "... had no leisure to form any scheme of conduct..."[9]
Sense and Sensibility, Volume the Third, Chapter 13, Narrator on Edward leaving Oxford

She didn't plan ahead

"... the rest of her life was at such a distance as to excite but little interest."[6]
Northanger Abbey, Chapter 17, Narrator on Catherine's life after Bath

Happiness & Gratitude

Happiness

She tried to keep things positive
She "...spared no exertions to maintain this happier flow of ideas ..."[1]
Emma, Chapter 1, Narrator on Emma

It's no big deal
"Very little apology could be requisite..."[3]
The Watsons, Emma to Elizabeth about Elizabeth going to the assembly instead of Emma

It cheered them up
"It was a most delightful reanimation of exhausted spirits."[1]
Emma, Chapter 23, Narrator on Emma encountering the Westons

She was in a good mood
Her "... spirits were mounted quite up to happiness."[1]
Emma, Chapter 23, Narrator on Emma encountering the Westons & hearing about Frank

Happily
"... with more thorough gaiety..."[1]
Emma, Chapter 53, Narrator on Emma considering the family's reaction to her engagement to Mr. Knightley

Brief happiness
"A short period of exquisite felicity..."[7]
Persuasion, Chapter 4, Narrator on Anne's engagement to Wentworth

All's well that ends well

"... as the effect was joyful, the cause could scarcely be lamented."[10]
Jack and Alice, Chapter 7, Narrator on Jack's death

They make a happy couple

"It was a union of the highest promise of felicity..."[1]
Emma, Chapter 53, Narrator on Mr. Weston's thoughts on Emma marrying Mr. Knightley

She was light-hearted

"... she possessed such a fund of vivacity and good humour as could only be damped by some very serious vexation."[10]
Catherine, Narrator on Catherine

What a fun summer

"I have seldom spent three months more agreeably than those which have just flown away."[3]
Lady Susan, Chapter 2, Lady Susan Vernon to Mrs. Johnson

I am proud of myself

"I commend my own conduct in this affair extremely, and regard it as a very happy instance of circumspection."[3]
Lady Susan, Chapter 7, Lady Susan Vernon to Mrs. Johnson

I was so happy, I couldn't move

"...I remained in the same spot, overpowered by wonder of a most agreeable sort indeed..."[3]
Lady Susan, Chapter 23, Mrs. Vernon to Lady De Courcy

It makes me really happy

It "... exalts me to the utmost pinnacle of human felicity, & makes me bask in the sunshine of Prosperity..."[2]

Jane Austen in a letter to Cassandra, Tuesday, January 8, 1799, about being able to mail off the letter

She was happy

She "... was all joyous delight..."[5]

Mansfield Park, Chapter 21, Narrator on Mrs. Norris after Maria's wedding

It's a good thing

It is "... a circumstance from which I derive ... pleasing reflections..."[2]

Jane Austen in a letter to Cassandra, Monday, November 30, 1800, about the purchase of muslin for a frock

I'm proud of it

"... it has ... opened to me a fresh source of self-congratulation..."[2]

Jane Austen in a letter to Cassandra, Monday, November 30, 1800, about the purchase of muslin for a frock

It'll be a lot of fun

"... there are to be ... Felicities of all kinds."[2]

Jane Austen in a letter to Cassandra, Friday, may 31, 1811, about a gathering the following Tuesday on Selbourne Common

All sorts of fun

"... everything that can be imagined agreable."[2]

Jane Austen in a letter to Cassandra, Friday, May 31, 1811, about Anna's evening with the Miss Middletons

She felt good about herself

"... her spirits were in as happy a flutter as vanity and pride could furnish..."[5]

Mansfield Park, Chapter 8, Narrator on Maria upon seeing Sotherton

This is nice

"Here's what may tranquillize every care, and lift the heart to rapture!"[5]
Mansfield Park, Chapter 11, Fanny to Edmund about the evening scenery

"... her imagination took a rapid flight over its attendant felicities."[6]
Northanger Abbey, Chapter 15, Narrator on Isabella upon receiving James' letter

He was happy

He "... gave every proof on his side of equal satisfaction..."[6]
Northanger Abbey, Chapter 7, Narrator on James & Catherine meeting in Bath

He "... was no skulker in joy."[6]
Northanger Abbey, Chapter 15, Narrator on John Thorpe upon Isabella's engagement

I can't wait 'til tomorrow night

"... the evening of the following day was now the object of expectation, the future good."[6]
Northanger Abbey, Chapter 10, Narrator on Catherine's expectation of seeing the Tilneys at the ball

It just doesn't get any better than this

"... it did not appear to her that life could supply any greater felicity."[6]
Northanger Abbey, Chapter 10, Narrator on Catherine escaping John Thorpe to dance with Mr. Tilney

She stayed positive

"...her cheerfulness and mental alacrity did not fail her..."[7]
Persuasion, Chapter 24, Narrator Mrs. Smith

Calmly

"... without shewing the smallest propensity towards any unpleasant vivacity..."[6]
Northanger Abbey, Chapter 9, Narrator on John Thorpe's horse

I'm okay

"... I do not feel so very, very much afflicted as one would have thought."[6]
Northanger Abbey, Chapter 25, Catherine to Mr. Tilney & Eleanor about losing Isabelle as a friend

Good feelings

"... those agreeable sensations..."[7]
Persuasion, Chapter 17, Narrator on Anne being complimented by Mr. Elliot

They had to contain their happiness

"There could only be a most proper alacrity, a most obliging compliance for public view; and smile reined in and spirits dancing in private rapture."[7]
Persuasion, Chapter 23, Narrator on Wentworth escorting Anne

You'd never know he was so happy

He was "... very laconic in his expressions of pleasure..."[8]
Pride and Prejudice, Chapter 12, Narrator on Mr. Bennet's reaction to Jane & Elizabeth's return

They looked forward to it

"The prospect of such delights was very cheering..."[8]
Pride and Prejudice, Chapter 15, Narrator on the invitation to dinner from Mrs. Philips

He bragged

"... he proceeded to inform them, with many rapturous expressions, of his happiness..."[8]
Pride and Prejudice, Chapter 23, Narrator on Mr. Collins' letter to Mr. Bennet

What you really want

Something "... so indispensably necessary to your future felicity."[9]
Sense and Sensibility, Volume the First, Chapter 4, Marianne to Elinor on Edward Ferrars' tastes in art

He liked to speed

"He always traveled remarkably expeditiously..."[10]
Memoirs of Mr. Clifford, Narrator on Mr. Clifford in his coach

Not bad, if I do say so myself

"Its effect... justifies some portion of vanity..."[3]
Lady Susan, Chapter 25, Lady Susan to Mrs. Johnson

No biggie

"... I do not consider as any Calamity."[2]
Jane Austen in a letter to Cassandra, Friday, December 28, 1798, about being invited to a ball by Lady Dortchester

"What a trifle it is in all its Bearings, to the really important points of one's existence..."[2]
Jane Austen in a letter to Frank, Saturday, September 25, 1813, about her fame in the wake of *Pride & Prejudice*

I hope you like them

"I hope you derive your full share of enjoyment from each."[2]
Jane Austen in a letter to Cassandra, Saturday, November 6, 1813, referring to the news & the weather

Everyone liked it

It was "... a pleasure to brighten every eye and occupy every fancy..."[6]
Northanger Abbey, Chapter 29, Narrator on Catherine arriving at Fullerton

---

Gratitude

"... the warm acknowledgement of peculiar obligation."[9]
Sense and Sensibility, Volume the Third, Chapter 10, Narrator on Marianne receiving Col. Brandon

She should have been grateful

"A large debt of gratitude was owing here ..."[1]
Emma, Chapter 1, Narrator on Emma and Miss Taylor.

She was thankful

Her "... gratitude ... was in the first style of guileless simplicity and warmth."[1]
Emma, Chapter 33, Narrator on Miss Bates' appreciation of Mrs. Elton's care for Jane

"Her grateful and gratified heart could hardly restrain its expressions within the language of tolerable calmness."[6]
Northanger Abbey, Chapter 17, Narrator on Catherine being invited to Northanger Abbey

"... her esteem for the general benevolence, and her gratitude for the particular friendship ... were strongly felt..."[9]
Sense and Sensibility, Volume the Third, Chapter 3, Narrator on Elinor receiving Col. Brandon's offer for Edward

I'm glad

"I rejoice in it very sincerely."[2]
Jane Austen in a letter to Cassandra, Thursday, June 30, 1808, about Elizabeth's tastes

Thanks a lot

"... I beg your acceptance of all the Thanks due on the occasion."[2]
Jane Austen in a letter to Cassandra, Tuesday, January 17, 1809, in gratitude for her last letter

"... my gratitude is warmly excited by such affectionate attention..."[8]
Pride and Prejudice, Chapter 22, Mr. Collins to Mr. Bennet on revisiting Longbourn

"... I ask, what am I to do with my gratitude?"[2]
Jane Austen in a letter to Cassandra, Monday, October 11, 1813, quoting *The History of Sir Charles Grandison*, by Samuel Richardson[2]

"I shall always think myself very much obliged to you."[9]
Sense and Sensibility, Volume the Third, Chapter 3, Elinor to Col. Brandon

She really appreciated it

"The value ... was most forcibly brought before her."[5]
Mansfield Park, Chapter 22, Narrator on Mary Crawford when Fanny visited

Thanks, it's just what I needed

"Your offer ... is very kind, & happens to be particularly adapted to my wants..."[2]
Jane Austen in a letter to Cassandra, Tuesday, January 17, 1809, some cravats

I'm thankful to him

"... I ... will value it very much as a proof of his affection..."[2]
Jane Austen in a letter to Cassandra, Tuesday, January 17, 1809, about her grandmother's appreciation of a footstool from William

How nice of you

It "... bears a stamp beyond all common Charity..."[2]
Jane Austen in a letter to Martha Lloyd, Sunday, November 29, 1812, about her care for sick children

"...you are everything that is generous and considerate..."[5]
Mansfield Park, Chapter 1, Mrs. Norris to Sir Thomas on his acquiescence to the plan of taking on Fanny

She says 'Thanks'

"I do not know when I have seen her so much struck by anybody's kindness as on this occasion."[2]
Jane Austen in a letter to Anna Lefroy, Sunday, June 23, 1816, about Cassy and a book

She "... spoke her pleasure aloud with such grateful surprize..."[6]
Northanger Abbey, Chapter 9, Narrator on Catherine after starting the ride with John Thorpe

He said thanks

He "... expressed himself on the occasion with becoming gratitude..."[6]
Northanger Abbey, Chapter 16, Narrator on James thanking his father for the living

A be thankful

"… to express a sense of obligation for the sentiments avowed…"[8]

Pride and Prejudice, Chapter 34, Elizabeth to Mr. Darcy in reply to his proposal

Congratulations

Congrats

"… it must have been a circumstance to increase every enjoyment you can have…"[2]

Jane Austen in a letter to Martha Lloyd, Friday, September 2, 1814, about Martha getting paid

Hope/Ambition & Despair

Hope & Ambition

Optimistically
"… without feeling one small foreboding of future misery to herself…"[6]
Northanger Abbey, Chapter 20, Narrator on Catherine's arrival at Northanger Abbey

Hopeful
"… with many cheerful prognostics…"[8]
Pride and Prejudice, Chapter 7, Narrator on Mrs. Bennet sending Jane out in the rain

It was her goal
"In the promotion of this object she was zealously active…"[9]
Sense and Sensibility, Volume the First, Chapter 8, Narrator on Mrs. Jennings wanting to marry off young people

She had to try
"… exertion was indispensably necessary…"[9]
Sense and Sensibility, Volume the First, Chapter 22, Narrator on Elinor keeping her strength with Lucy Steele

She had to work for it
"… it obliged her to unceasing exertion…"[9]
Sense and Sensibility, Volume the Second, Chapter 1, Narrator on Elinor concealing Lucy & Edward's engagement

She really wanted to do it

"She began ... seriously to turn her thoughts towards its accomplishment..."[9]
Sense and Sensibility, Volume the Third, Chapter 3, Narrator on Elinor wanting to leave London

Trying to believe

"... conning over every injunction of mistrust..."[9]
Sense and Sensibility, Volume the Third, Chapter 7, Narrator on Elinor and Marianne's improvement

We were confident

"... sanguine hopes were entertained..."[3]
The Watsons, Narrator on the Osbornes attending the winter assembly

Just about perfect

"... only too palpably desirable, natural, and probable..."[1]
Emma, Chapter 4, Narrator on Emma's designs for Harriet & Mr. Elton

She was hopeful

"... her heart under circumstances, which she chose to consider as peculiarly propitious..."[3]
The Watsons, Narrator on Margaret's expectations with Tom Musgrave

We're definitely doing it this time

"But now it was to be more resolutely undertaken..."[3]
Sanditon, Chapter 12, Narrator on Charlotte visiting Sanditon House

It was on her mind

"... in anticipation ... it became henceforth her prime object of interest..."[1]
Emma, Chapter 11, Narrator on Emma & her sister's visit

"To that point went ... every moment of involuntary absence of mind."[1]
Emma, Chapter 47, Narrator on Emma considering her own feelings for Mr. Knightley

Your plans

"... that scheme which ... doubtless ... possessed your imagination?"[10]
Love and Friendship, Letter 12th, Laura to Marianne quoting Laura to Cpt. M'Kenzie

I want it

"... I am quite dying of envy for it."[10]
Catherine, Camilla to Mrs. Stanley about Augusta Barlow's dress

Strong hope for her success

"...the most flattering prognostics of her future renown."[3]
Lady Susan, Chapter 19, Lady Susan to Mrs. Johnson

There's no point in thinking about it

"It was a subject, in short, on which reflection would be long indulged, and must be unavailing."[8]
Pride and Prejudice, Chapter 24, Narrator on Mr. Bingley's thoughts on Jane

Don't give up

"I insist upon your persevering in your design..."[2]
Jane Austen in a letter to Cassandra, Monday, December 24, 1798, about Cassandra buying a new gown

He didn't try real hard

"... he did not want it quite enough to make much trouble in effecting it..."[2]
Jane Austen in a letter to Cassandra, Tuesday, January 8, 1799, about an officer wanting to meet Jane at a ball

If all goes well

"If circumstances are favourable..."[2]
Jane Austen in a letter to Cassandra, Thursday, June 30, 1808, about the scheme to Beaulieu

The medication should help

"... the strong medicines requisite..." are "... promising to be effectual."[2]
Jane Austen in a letter to Cassandra, Monday, January 30, 1809, about Mrs. Cooke's illness

I hope she doesn't do anything embarrassing

"I hope she will not sully the respectable name she now bears."[2]
Jane Austen in a letter to Cassandra, Monday, January 30, 1809, about Jenny & her marriage

All or nothing

"Such half and half doings never prosper."[5]
Mansfield Park, Chapter 5, Mary Crawford to Thomas Bertram

She wished harm

She "... was not superior to the hope of some distressing end..."[5]
Mansfield Park, Chapter 17, Narrator on Julia's reaction to Henry Crawford's attentions to Maria

It's what she really wanted

It "... was the height of her ambition, and seemed to comprehend her greatest possibility of happiness."[5]
Mansfield Park, Chapter 27, Narrator on Fanny's hopes for the ball

She expected it to work

She "... was not less sanguine as to its effect..."[5]
Mansfield Park, Chapter 32, Narrator on Fanny and her letter to Mary Crawford

She didn't want to

"She had hardly even attained the wish to do it."[5]

Mansfield Park, Chapter 32, Narrator on Fanny not interrupting Sir Thomas' lecture

She wouldn't back out now

"... she would not, upon any account, retract."[6]

Northanger Abbey, Chapter 13, Narrator on Catherine's walk with the Tilney's

His confident hopes

"All his sanguine expectations..."[7]

Persuasion, Chapter 4, Narrator on Wentworth's prospects

Confident faith in the future

"... a cheerful confidence in futurity, against that over-anxious caution which seems to insult exertion and distrust Providence!"[7]

Persuasion, Chapter 4, Narrator on Anne's feelings

She was optimistic

"...here was that elasticity of mind, that disposition to be comforted, that power of turning readily from evil to good, and of finding employment which carried her out of herself, which was from nature alone."[7]

Persuasion, Chapter 17, Narrator on Mrs. Smith's disposition

She was "... more ready to see alleviations of the evil before her..."[1]

Emma, Chapter 16, Narrator on Emma thinking about telling Harriet about Mr. Elton

Her broken dreams

"… the extinction of all her dearest hopes…"[9]
Sense and Sensibility, Volume the Second, Chapter 1, Narrator on Elinor losing Edward Ferrars

I doubt it

"… at present I cannot indulge any expectation of it."[2]
Jane Austen in a letter to Cassandra, Saturday, November 17, 1798, quoting a letter Mrs. Lefroy received about the Austens

It's unlikely

It "… may be too reasonably doubted."[2]
Jane Austen in a letter to Martha Lloyd, Wednesday, November 12, 1800, about the revival of health at Manydown

I gave it a shot

I "… did everything that extraordinary Abilities could be supposed to compass…"[2]
Jane Austen in a letter to Cassandra, Monday, November 30, 1800, about observing Mrs. Poore & her mother

She tried not to think about it

"… she felt quite unequal to surmising … anything more."[5]
Mansfield Park, Chapter 22, Narrator on Fanny in conversation with Mary Crawford about Edmund

Improvements & Deteriorations

Improvements

Her problems cleared up

"... her difficulties were instantly obviated..."[9]

Sense and Sensibility, Volume the Third, Chapter 7, Narrator on Elinor when Col. Brandon volunteered to fetch Mrs. Dashwood

To calm her down

"... to fill her heart with sensations of exquisite comfort..."[9]

Sense and Sensibility, Volume the Third, Chapter 7, Narrator on Elinor and Marianne's recovery

Helping

"...supplying every succor..."[9]

Sense and Sensibility, Volume the Third, Chapter 7, Narrator on Elinor nursing Marianne

It's worth the effort

It "... is worth a great deal more than any little exertion it needs."[1]

Emma, Chapter 23, Mr. Weston on Frank's early arrival

I hope it makes her feel better

"...I hope her engagement will have every alleviation that is possible..."[1]

Emma, Chapter 44, Emma to Miss Bates about Jane's position with Mrs. Smallridge

She learns from her mistakes

"...the lessons of her past folly might teach her humility and circumspection in future."[1]
Emma, Chapter 54, Narrator on Emma growing to deserve Mr. Knightley

Things were going well

"...my mind was entirely satisfied with the posture of affairs."[3]
Lady Susan, Chapter 22, Lady Susan to Mrs. Johnson

I am pro-education

"... I am an advocate for the prevailing fashion of acquiring a perfect knowledge of all languages, arts, and sciences."[3]
Lady Susan, Chapter 7, Lady Susan Vernon to Mrs. Johnson

Things are really looking up

"...matters have now taken so favourable a turn..."[3]
Lady Susan, Chapter 23, Mrs. Vernon to Lady De Courcy

I'll make it up to her

"She shall have all the retribution in my power to make..."[3]
Lady Susan, Chapter 24, Mrs. Vernon to Lady De Courcy

He can finally relax

"... he has now a little intermission of his excessive solicitude..."[2]
Jane Austen in a letter to Cassandra, Sunday, June 26, 1808, about Mr. Whitfield's concerns for his wife

She's doing a lot better than the doctor thought

"... her amendment has already surpassed the expectation of the Physician..."[2]
Jane Austen in a letter to Cassandra, Tuesday, January 10, 1809, about the health of Cassandra's godmother

She's feeling better

"She is wonderfully recovered from the severity of her … complaint."[2]
Jane Austen in a letter to Frank, Saturday, September 25, 1813, about Mme. Bigeon

It was a learning experience

"It was a medicinal project upon … understanding, which he must consider as at present diseased."[5]
Mansfield Park, Chapter 37, Narrator on Sir Thomas' scheme to send Fanny to Portsmouth

It was the only thing that made her feel better

It "… was the nearest to administering comfort of anything within the current of her thoughts."[5]
Mansfield Park, Chapter 42, Narrator on Fanny considering the improvements in Henry Crawford

She finally pulled herself together

At length, a something like composure succeeded."[5]
Mansfield Park, Chapter 43, Narrator on Fanny waiting for a letter from Edmund

Motivate her

"… strive to rouse her … to … exertion…"[9]
Sense and Sensibility, Volume the First, Chapter 1, Narrator on Elinor & Mrs. Dashwood

It changed her mind

It "… militated against all her established ideas…"[9]
Sense and Sensibility, Volume the First, Chapter 3, Narrator on Mrs. Dashwood's opinion of Edward Ferrars

I get it

It is "... brought more within my comprehension."[9]

Sense and Sensibility, Volume the Third, Chapter 1, Marianne to Elinor on her attitude toward Edward's engagement

When things calmed down

"... after the first ebullition of surprise and satisfaction was over..."[9]

Sense and Sensibility, Volume the Third, Chapter 4, Narrator on Elinor & Mrs. Jennings after discovering their misunderstanding

To make him less gullible

"... to upbraid him from his easy credulity."[1]

Emma, Chapter 42, Narrator on Mr. Woodhouse being invited to Donwell for the strawberry party

She was forgiven

She "... was now spoken of with compassionate allowances."[1]

Emma, Chapter 45, Narrator on Mrs. Churchill's death

She finally got what she wanted

"... the unwearied diligence with which she had every day wished for the same thing was at length to have its just reward..."[6]

Northanger Abbey, Chapter 4, Narrator on Mrs. Allen's wish to know more people in Bath

He made improvements

"... when the genius of others had failed, his own had often produced the perfection wanted."[6]

Northanger Abbey, Chapter 23, Narrator on General Tilney's improvements to the abbey kitchen

Things slowly got better

"… the lenient hand of time did much for her by insensible gradations…"[6]
Northanger Abbey, Chapter 25, Narrator on Catherine after being caught by Mr. Tilney

Learn from your mistakes

"… an occasional memento of past folly, however painful, might not be without use."[6]
Northanger Abbey, Chapter 25, Narrator on Catherine after being caught by Mr. Tilney

Education

"… improvement to be engrafted on what nature had given…"[1]
Emma, Chapter 20, Narrator on Jane's childhood

Deteriorations

Things got worse

"But the day did not close so auspiciously as it began."[9]
Sense and Sensibility, Volume the Third, Chapter 7, Narrator on Marianne's illness

It's bad for you

It "… will, in the end … prove destructive to your constitution."[10]
Love and Friendship, Letter 14th, Laura to Marianne quoting Sophia about fainting

What a huge oversight

"Here is some great misapprehension which must be rectified."[5]
Mansfield Park, Chapter 32, Sir Thomas to Fanny about having a fire in her room

She has changed

"...she is quite an altered creature."[9]

Sense and Sensibility, Volume the Second, Chapter 7, Mrs. Jennings to Elinor about Marianne

She thought it was a bad influence

She "... was disposed to think the influence very much at war with all respectable attachments."[5]

Mansfield Park, Chapter 45, Narrator on Fanny's opinion of her cousins in London

Weather, Seasons, & Nature

Spring had sprung

"… every day was adding to the verdure of the early trees."[8]
Pride and Prejudice, Chapter 35, Narrator on Rosings Park in the spring

It's been nice out

"The weather does not know how to be otherwise than fine."[2]
Jane Austen in a letter to Cassandra, Saturday, October 25, 1800

It only rained a little

"… our share of the Showers was very trifling…"[2]
Jane Austen in a letter to Cassandra, Thursday, May 20, 1813

I enjoy nature

"… to sit in the shade on a fine day and look upon verdure, is the most perfect refreshment."[5]
Mansfield Park, Chapter 9, Fanny to Edmund & Mary Crawford about leaving her alone to rest

"One cannot fix one's eye on the commonest natural production without finding food for a rambling fancy."[5]
Mansfield Park, Chapter 22, Fanny to Mary Crawford on the scenery around the Parsonage

It's dusk

"The shades of Evening are descending…"[2]
Jane Austen in a letter to Cassandra, Saturday, November 6, 1813

The mood was set

"The season, the scene, the air, were all favourable to tenderness and sentiment."[5]
Mansfield Park, Chapter 7, Narrator on Edmund watching Mary Crawford play the harp

It hasn't been too hot

"The weather can hardly have incommoded you by its' heat."[2]
Jane Austen in a letter to Martha Lloyd, Friday, September 2, 1814

Family, Marriage, & Parenting/Parent-Child Relations

Marriage & Family

Their happy marriage

"… their career of conjugal felicity…"[5]

Mansfield Park, Chapter 1, Narrator on Mr. & Mrs. Norris

Everyone thought she had a happy marriage

"… no one would have supposed … that she had ever heard of conjugal infelicity in her life…"[5]

Mansfield Park, Chapter 21, Narrator on Mrs. Norris after Maria's wedding

Family strife

"…unwelcome sensations arising from family affairs…"[7]

Persuasion, Chapter 1, Narrator on Elliot household

This chaotic house is stressful

She "… would have deemed such a domestic hurricane a bad restorative of the nerves…"[7]

Persuasion, Chapter 14, Narrator on Uppercross with the Musgrove and Harville children

He is a family man

He has "... a value for all the felicities of domestic life..."[7]
Persuasion, Chapter 16, Narrator on Mr. Elliot

We sisters have to stick together through this

"But we must stem the tide of malice, and pour into the wounded bosoms of each other, the balm of sisterly consolation."[8]
Pride and Prejudice, Chapter 47, Mary to Elizabeth, concerning Lydia's elopement

He had a happy home

"... he found no inconsiderable degree of domestic felicity."[9]
Sense and Sensibility, Volume the Third, Chapter 13, Narrator on Willoughby's marriage

Divorce

"... the sad end of all ... connubial happiness..."[4]
Lesley Castle, Margaret to Charlotte on Lesley when Louisa left

I am no home wrecker

"...I may not in any way be instrumental in separating a family so affectionately attached to each other."[3]
Lady Susan, Chapter 25, Lady Susan to Mrs. Johnson

She's looking to get married

"... she has a matrimonial project in view..."[2]
Jane Austen in a letter to Cassandra, Wednesday, June 19, 1799, about Miss Pearson

He was hen-pecked

"He acquiesced in all her decisions..."[9]
Sense and Sensibility, Volume the First, Chapter 10, Narrator on Willoughby with Marianne

Children/Child Rearing/Child-Parent Relations

She looks pregnant

"... from her appearance I suspect her to be in the family way."[2]

Jane Austen in a letter to Cassandra, Thursday, September 16, 1813, about Mrs. Tilson[2]

She was sheltered

She had "... very little to distress or vex her." [1]

Emma, Chapter 1, Narrator's description of Emma Woodhouse.

Spoiled little girls

"...daughters of a most affectionate, indulgent father ..."[1]

Emma, Chapter 1, Narrator's description of the Woodhouse family

She wasn't strict

"...the mildness of her temper had hardly allowed her to impose any restraint ..."[1]

Emma, Chapter 1, Narrator's description of Miss Taylor

Spoiling her kids

Her "... material solicitude for the immediate enjoyment of her little ones..."[1]

Emma, Chapter 11, Narrator on Isabella

"With her children they were in continual raptures, extolling their beauty, courting their notice, and humouring all their whims..."[9]

Sense and Sensibility, Volume the First, Chapter 21, Narrator on the Miss Steeles and the Middleton children

She spoiled her

"To her she was most injudiciously indulgent."[5]
Mansfield Park, Chapter 39, Narrator on Mrs. Price favoring Betsy

You never listened to Dad

"... I entirely acquit you of ever having willingly contributed to the satisfaction of your father."[10]
Love and Friendship, Letter 7th, Laura to Marianne, quoting Edward to Augusta

They flew the nest

They "... disentangled themselves from the shackles of parental authority..."[10]
Love and Friendship, Letter 9th, Laura to Marianne about Augustus & Sophia

He stole from his dad's desk

He "... gracefully purloined from his ... father's escritoire..."[10]
Love and Friendship, Letter 9th, Laura to Marianne about Augustus

A bad wife and mother

She, "... who had so wantonly disgraced the Maternal character and so openly violated the conjugal Duties..."[4]
Lesley Castle, Margaret to Charlotte about Louisa

A mother's love

"The sacred impulse of maternal affection."[3]
Lady Susan, Chapter 2, Lady Susan Vernon to Mrs. Vernon.

I was a spoiled and lazy child and so I now come off crude

"I was so much indulged in my infant years that I was never obliged to attend to anything, and consequently am without the accomplishments which are now necessary to finish a pretty woman." [3]

Lady Susan, Chapter 7, Lady Susan Vernon to Mrs. Johnson

To go against her mother's wishes

To have "...any claim to the indulgence of her notions at the expense of her mother's inclinations." [3]

Lady Susan, Chapter 25, Lady Susan to Mrs. Johnson

When you get married and have kids

When you are "... all settled down into conjugal & maternal affections." [2]

Jane Austen in a letter to Fanny Knight, Thursday, February 20, 1817, about Fanny settling down

He didn't scold his other kids

"He did not enter into any remonstrance with his other children..." [5]

Mansfield Park, Chapter 20, Narrator on Sir Thomas not bringing up the play

She was becoming rebellious

"She was less and less able to endure the restraint which her father imposed." [5]

Mansfield Park, Chapter 21, Narrator on Maria's reasons for marrying Mr. Rushworth

His mother was worried

"The real solicitude now awakened in the maternal bosom was not soon over." [5]

Mansfield Park, Chapter 44, Narrator on Lady Bertram's concern over Tom's illness

He let his kids run free

"... he was not in the least addicted to locking up his daughters."[6]
Northanger Abbey, Chapter 1, Narrator on Mr. Morland

She bragged about her kids

"... she expatiated on the talents of her sons, and the beauty of her daughters..."[6]
Northanger Abbey, Chapter 4, Narrator on Mrs. Thorpe in her first encounter with Mrs. Allen

She had to listen to a mother go on and on about her kids

She "... was forced to sit and appear to listen to all these maternal effusions..."[6]
Northanger Abbey, Chapter 4, Narrator on Mrs. Allen's first conversation with Mrs. Thorpe

He was hard on his kids

He "... seemed always a check on his children's spirits..."[6]
Northanger Abbey, Chapter 20, Narrator on General Tilney

To spoil her

To make "... the study of her comfort and amusement ... their chief object..."[6]
Northanger Abbey, Chapter 28, Narrator on General Tilney's orders to Mr. Tilney & Eleanor in his absence

His parent's approval

"... he was sanctioned by parental authority in his present application."[6]
Northanger Abbey, Chapter 30, Narrator on General Tilney's thoughts on Mr. Tilney's proposal

In trouble with the parents

"... under every disadvantage of disapprobation at home..."[7]
Persuasion, Chapter 4, Narrator on Lady Russell's dislike of Wentworth

Protecting against (a bully)

"... sedulously guarding from the tyranny of..."[7] a bully

Persuasion, Chapter 14, Narrator on Mrs. Musgrove with the children

Childish mistakes

"... erring in the heyday of youth."[7]

Persuasion, Chapter 16, Narrator on Mr. Elliot & Lady Russell

He disobeyed his parents

"... he does seem to have had some filial scruples on that head..."[8]

Pride and Prejudice, Chapter 13, Mr. Bennet on Mr. Collins ending his father's feud

He loved kids

"... the cheerfulness of ... children added a relish to his existence."[9]

Sense and Sensibility, Volume the First, Chapter 1, Narrator on Old Mr. Dashwood

Relationships

Affection

A passing fancy

"... only a slight, thin sort of inclination..."[8]
Pride and Prejudice, Chapter 9, Elizabeth to Mr. Darcy on the effects of poetry

He obviously likes her

"... nothing could more agreeably denote his wish of ... securing her affection."[1]
Emma, Chapter 24, Narrator on Frank's treatment of Mrs. Weston

He was glad to see her

He "... looked with most unfeigned satisfaction at her..."[1]
Emma, Chapter 4, Narrator on Robert Martin seeing Harriet on a walk with Emma

I like it

"I am dotingly fond of ..."[1] it.
Emma, Chapter 32, Mrs. Elton to Emma about music

A person she liked

A person "... on whom she would have lavished every distinction of regard..."[1]
Emma, Chapter 45, Narrator on Emma's regard for Jane

I love them

"... I declare I quite dote upon them -."[10]
Catherine, Camilla to Catherine about the Dudleys

Really, really likes me

Is "...impressed with the deepest conviction of my merit..."3

Lady Susan, Chapter 16, Lady Susan to Mrs. Johnson

They liked each other

They were ... "very mutually attached ..."1

Emma, Chapter 1, Narrator on Emma and Miss Taylor

He took a keen interest in her

He "...watched her with so much tender solicitude..."3

Lady Susan, Chapter 17, Mrs. Vernon to Lady De Courcy

Happily seeing his mood

"...observing his countenance with exultation..."3

Lady Susan, Chapter 17, Mrs. Vernon to Lady De Courcy

She was really into him

"...her eyes fixed on his face with a remarkable expression of pensive admiration."3

Lady Susan, Chapter 18, Mrs. Vernon to Lady De Courcy

"Her sentiments toward him were compounded of all that was respectful, grateful, confiding, and tender."5

Mansfield Park, Chapter 4, Narrator on Fanny's feelings for Edmund

A mad crush

"...the tyrannic influence of youth on youth ..."1

Emma, Chapter 2, Narrator on Mr. Weston and Miss Taylor

It was just a crush

"It was a little fever of admiration..."7

Persuasion, Chapter 10, Narrator on the Miss Musgroves' feelings for Wentworth

Blinded by love

She "...had such an affection for her as could never find fault."[1]
Emma, Chapter 1, Narrator on Miss Taylor and Emma

To wish they were not dating

"...to lament the degree of intimacy subsisting between them..."[3]
Lady Susan, Chapter 15, Mrs. Vernon to Lady De Courcy

They were close

"... they ... looked on each other with something more than bare politeness."[10]
Frederic and Elfrida, Chapter 1, Narrator on Frederic & Elfrida

You really dig him

"... your heart has not been able to withstand the fascinating charms of this young man..."[10]
Jack and Alice, Chapter 2, Lady Williams to Alice about Charles Adams

I really like him

I like him "... to the utmost, to the very top of the Glass, quite brimful."[2]
Jane Austen in a letter to Fanny Knight, Thursday, February 20, 1817, about Henry

It was just brotherly love

"... it was con amore fraternal and no other."[5]
Mansfield Park, Chapter 29, Narrator on Fanny missing William and not Henry Crawford

It was a one-sided relationship

"On his side the inclination was stronger, on hers less equivocal."[5]
Mansfield Park, Chapter 37, Narrator on Edmund & Mary Crawford

She still liked him

"… his impression on her fancy was not suffered … to weaken."[6]

Northanger Abbey, Chapter 5, Narrator on Catherine's thoughts of Mr. Tilney

Working hard for someone

"…exertions of loyalty…"[7]

Persuasion, Chapter 1, Narrator

They were in love

"… there could have been no two hearts so open, no tastes so similar, no feelings so in unison, no countenances so beloved."[7]

Persuasion, Chapter 8, Narrator on Anne & Wentworth during the engagement

They seemed to like each other

"…there had been a considerable appearance of attachment…"[7]

Persuasion, Chapter 9, Narrator on Henrietta & Charles Hayter

She was faithful

"… her feelings were still adverse to any man save one…"[7]

Persuasion, Chapter 17, Narrator on Anne's attachment to Wentworth

He won't get over her

"A man does not recover from such a devotion of the heart to such a woman! He ought not; he does not."[7]

Persuasion, Chapter 20, Wentworth on Benwick's attachment to Fanny Harville

She was ready to win him over

She "… prepared in the highest spirits for the conquest of all that remained unsubdued in his heart…"[8]
Pride and Prejudice, Chapter 18, Narrator on Elizabeth preparing to meet Mr. Wickham at the Netherfield ball

He's dating her

"… he will have frequent opportunity now of seeing her on the most intimate footing…"[8]
Pride and Prejudice, Chapter 21, Caroline Bingley in a letter to Jane on Mr. Bingley & Georgiana Darcy

She cared about him

"… there was a solicitude, an interest which she felt must ever attach her to him with a most sincere regard…"[8]
Pride and Prejudice, Chapter 27, Narrator on Elizabeth's connection to Mr. Wickham

She grew to like him

"The respect created by the conviction of his valuable qualities … had for some time ceased to be repugnant to her feelings…"[8]
Pride and Prejudice, Chapter 44, Narrator on Elizabeth's changing feelings toward Mr. Darcy

Done out of love

"… urged by a strong impulse of affectionate sensibility…"[9]
Sense and Sensibility, Volume the Second, Chapter 12, Narrator on Marianne when Elinor was slighted

Moving too fast (in a relationship)

"… rushing into intimacy on so slight an acquaintance."[3]
The Watsons, Narrator on Emma's apprehension in meeting people at the assembly

They were a good match

"… it would appear that their dispositions were as exactly fitted to make them blessed in each other…"[5]

Mansfield Park, Chapter 34, Narrator on Edmund's opinion of Fanny & Henry Crawford

Like peas and carrots

"… any couple … who were attracted by resemblance of disposition…"[9]

Sense and Sensibility, Volume the First, Chapter 3, Narrator on Elinor & Edward Ferrars

There were mixed feelings about her

"Many were the eyes, and various the degrees of approbation with which she was examined."[3]

The Watsons, Narrator on the visitors to Mrs. Edwards after the assembly examining Emma

Admiration

He was impressed

"…his faculties were roused into admiration…"[7]

Persuasion, Chapter 1, Narrator on Sir Walter Elliot

To impress him

"…to excite his esteem."[7]

Persuasion, Chapter 1, Narrator on Anne's features in her father's eyes

Thoughts of romance

"Prettier musings of high-wrought love and eternal constancy…"[7]

Persuasion, Chapter 21, Narrator on Anne's thoughts in Bath

He respected her

"Her character was now fixed on his mind as perfection itself, maintaining the loveliest medium of fortitude and gentleness..."[7]
Persuasion, Chapter 23, Narrator on Wentworth and Anne's conversation

She didn't think she deserved him

"She hardly knew how to suppose that she could be an object of admiration to so great a man..."[8]
Pride and Prejudice, Chapter 10, Narrator on Elizabeth's notice of Mr. Darcy's attentions

They were as awesome as people said they'd be

"... he found them as handsome and amiable as they were represented by common report."[8]
Pride and Prejudice, Chapter 15, Narrator on Mr. Collins' reaction to the Misses Bennet

He impressed her

"... she... could not seriously picture to herself a more agreeable or estimable man."[7]
Persuasion, Chapter 16, Narrator on Mr. Elliot & Lady Russell

He thought she was swell

"... he had never seen any thing but affability in her."[8]
Pride and Prejudice, Chapter 14, Narrator on Mr. Collins' praise of Lady Catherine

They grew to like her

"The prejudices which had met her at first ... were all dissipated."[3]
Sanditon, Chapter 3, Narrator on Clara & the people of Sanditon

Her admiration for him

"... the animated contemplation of his worth..."[1]
Emma, Chapter 54, Narrator on Emma's thoughts on Mr. Knightley compared to Frank

You do so many kind things

"I admire the activity of your benevolence..."[8]

Pride and Prejudice, Chapter 7, Mary to Elizabeth on Elizabeth walking to Netherfield

Maybe he's just trying to impress us

"I do not know whether he has any design of ingratiating himself with either of us..."[1]

Emma, Chapter 4, Emma to Harriet about Mr. Elton

He kissed up

He "... had been pointedly attentive."[7]

Persuasion, Chapter 14, Narrator on Mr. Elliot's visits to Camden Place

Light flirting

"... little gallantries and allusions had been dropped, but nothing serious."[1]

Emma, Chapter 10, Narrator on Mr. Elton & Harriet at the vicarage

He kept flirting with her

He was "... continually obtruding his ... countenance on her notice and solicitously addressing her upon every occasion."[1]

Emma, Chapter 14, Narrator on Mr. Elton's attentions to Emma during the Westons' party

Trying to please each other

"... each to endeavor to give the other no cause for wishing that he or she had bestowed themselves elsewhere..."[6]

Northanger Abbey, Chapter 10, Mr. Tilney to Catherine about the responsibilities of a dance partner

She started to flirt around

"A short absence from home had left his fair one unguarded by his attentions..."[7]
Persuasion, Chapter 9, Narrator on Henrietta & Charles Hayter

Free to flirt

"... at liberty to exert his most open powers of pleasing."[7]
Persuasion, Chapter 17, Narrator on Mr. Elliot courting Anne

She wanted to check him out

She "... was not sorry to have such an opportunity of survey..."[1]
Emma, Chapter 4, Narrator on Emma seeing Robert Martin

She "... soon made her quick eye acquainted with..."[1] him.
Emma, Chapter 4, Narrator on Emma seeing Robert Martin

I didn't pretend to be bold just to flirt with girls

"... I did not assume the character of needless precipitance merely to shew off before the ladies."[8]
Pride and Prejudice, Chapter 10, Mr. Bingley to Mr. Darcy, defending his earlier comments

Showing that he's into her

"... marking his animated admiration of her..."[9]
Sense and Sensibility, Volume the First, Chapter 11, Narrator on Willoughby with Marianne

Her obvious flirting

"... the most pointed assurance of her affection."[9]
Sense and Sensibility, Volume the First, Chapter 11, Narrator on Marianne with Willoughby

Confident women often seem flirtatious

"One is apt, I believe, to connect assurance of manner with coquetry." [3]

Lady Susan, Chapter 6, Mrs. Vernon to Mr. De Courcy

To seduce her

"... to excite the first ardours of her young, unsophisticated mind!" [5]

Mansfield Park, Chapter 24, Narrator on Henry Crawford's desire for Fanny's love

Professions of Love or Admiration

"You pierce my soul. I am half agony, half hope."

Persuasion, Chapter 23, Wentworth's letter to Anne

"Too good, too excellent creature!"

Persuasion, Chapter 23, Wentworth's letter to Anne

"I offer myself to you again with a heart even more your own than when you almost broke it..."

Persuasion, Chapter 23, Wentworth's letter to Anne

"You do believe that there is true attachment and constancy among men. Believe it to be most fervent, most undeviating..."

Persuasion, Chapter 23, Wentworth's letter to Anne

"In vain I have struggled. It will not do. My feelings will not be repressed. You must allow me to tell you how ardently I admire and love you."

Pride and Prejudice, Chapter 34, Mr. Darcy to Elizabeth

"... she was elevated beyond the common timidity of her mind by the flow of her love..."
Mansfield Park, Chapter 24, Narrator Fanny while William was visiting
"You have some touches of the angel in you..."
Mansfield Park, Chapter 34, Henry Crawford to Fanny

"His happiness in knowing himself to have been so long the beloved of such a heart, must have been great enough to warrant any strength of language in which he could clothe it to her or to himself..."
Mansfield Park, Chapter 48, Narrator on Edmund discovering Fanny's affections

You "... convinced me of your being superior in good-nature yourself to all the rest of the world."
Northanger Abbey, Chapter 16, Mr. Tilney to Catherine
"An humble admirer now addresses you."
Amelia Webster, Letter the Sixth, George Hervey to Amelia Webster (*Juvenilia*)

Her "... feelings ... were at that time so exquisite, and the tenderness she felt ... so poignant..."
Love and Friendship, Letter 13th, Laura to Marianne about Sophia & Augustus (*Juvenilia*)

Absence or Loss of Affection

He could tell she wasn't into him

He "... watched her through the fluctuations of this speech and saw no alarming symptoms of love."[1]
Emma, Chapter 4, Narrator on Emma listening to Harriet talk of Robert Martin

She needs a good man

"It would not be a bad thing for her to be very much in love with a proper object."[1]
Emma, Chapter 5, Mr. Knightley to Mrs. Weston about Emma

He didn't sound like he cared for her

"... she could hardly devise any set of expressions or fancy any tone of voice less allied with real love."[1]
Emma, Chapter 16, Narrator on Emma and Mr. Elton's talk of Harriet

You're not attracted to older women

"... you may choose to question the allurements of a lady no longer young."[3]
Lady Susan, Chapter 6, Mrs. Vernon to Mr. De Courcy

I care what he thinks

"... the loss of his valued esteem I am...ill-fitted to endure..."[3]
Lady Susan, Chapter 30, Lady Susan Vernon to Mr. De Courcy

I didn't like him

He "...has left a strong impression in his disfavor with me."[7]
Persuasion, Chapter 14, Lady Russell on Mr. Elliot

She grew to like him even less

Her "... dislike of his general behavior, was sharpened into particular resentment..."[8]
Pride and Prejudice, Chapter 3, Narrator on Mrs. Bennet and Mr. Darcy at the assembly

She still disliked him

She "... remained with no very cordial feelings towards him."[8]
Pride and Prejudice, Chapter 3, Narrator on Elizabeth and Mr. Darcy at the assembly

I won't give him a good reason to hate me

"I always delight in overthrowing those kinds of schemes, and cheating a person of their premeditated contempt."[8]
Pride and Prejudice, Chapter 10, Elizabeth to Mr. Darcy on ignoring his request to dance

He stopped caring

"His apparent partiality had subsided…"[8]
Pride and Prejudice, Chapter 26, Narrator on Mr. Wickham's regard for Elizabeth

Leading her on

"… trying to engage her regard, without a thought of returning it."[9]
Sense and Sensibility, Volume the Third, Chapter 8, Willoughby to Elinor about Marianne

I don't care to know him

He "… gives me very little inclination for his acquaintance."[3]
The Watsons, Emma to Elizabeth about Tom Musgrave

She didn't try to impress him

"She liked him too little to care for his approbation."[8]
Pride and Prejudice, Chapter 10, Narrator on Elizabeth's notice of Mr. Darcy's attentions

He grew to dislike her

"… she had been regularly losing ground in his esteem…"[5]
Mansfield Park, Chapter 48, Narrator on Mrs. Norris & Sir Thomas

She didn't care

She "… replied … with the most placid indifference."[6]

Northanger Abbey, Chapter 9, Narrator on Mrs. Allen reply to Catherine's request for advice

I really hate him

"...the extent of my aversion is not to be estimated." [3]

Lady Susan, Chapter 29, Lady Susan Vernon to Mrs. Johnson

He hides his feelings

"He is not a young man with whom one can be intimately acquainted in a short time..." [9]

Sense and Sensibility, Volume the Third, Chapter 3, Col. Brandon to Elinor about Edward Ferrars

Visiting, Time Together, & Separations

Visiting & Spending Time Together

To hang out with her again

To "...give her pleasant society again."[1]
Emma, Chapter 1, Narrator on Emma and Isabella.

A chance to go out

"...the privilege of exchanging any vacant evening of his own blank solitude for the elegancies and society..."[1]
Emma, Chapter 3, Narrator on Mr. Elton

You wanna hang out with us?

"We shall be most happy to consider you as one of the party."[1]
Emma, Chapter 6, Emma to Mr. Elton inviting him to read for the sitting

I will get to know him

"... I shall gradually get intimately acquainted..."[1]
Emma, Chapter 10, Emma to Harriet about the area around the vicarage

She wanted him to come

"... she had particular pleasure ... in procuring him the proper invitation."[1]
Emma, Chapter 12, Narrator on Emma inviting Mr. Knightley to dinner

They enjoyed their private talks

Their "… uninterrupted communication … was one of the first gratifications of each."[1]
Emma, Chapter 14, Narrator on Emma & Mrs. Weston

He really wanted to come

"… it could not be fairly supposed that he had been ever voluntarily absenting himself…"[1]
Emma, Chapter 24, Narrator on Frank's interest in Highbury

Come visit me

"… how happy I should be to see you within these venerable Walls!"[4]
Lesley Castle, Margaret to Charlotte

I'll come visit you

"I can no longer refuse myself the pleasure of profiting by your kind invitation."[3]
Lady Susan, Chapter 1, Lady Susan Vernon to Mr. Vernon in accepting an invitation to visit.

I can't wait to chill with you

"I impatiently look forward to the hour when I shall be admitted into your delightful retirement."[3]
Lady Susan, Chapter 1, Lady Susan Vernon to Mr. Vernon.

I hope you'll have me

"It would indeed give me most painful sensations to know that it were not in your power to receive me."[3]
Lady Susan, Chapter 1, Lady Susan Vernon to Mr. Vernon.

Who knows how long it will last? (Referring to a visit)

"It is impossible to conjecture its length."[3]
Lady Susan, Chapter 3, Mrs. Vernon to Lady De Courcy.

She says she wants to meet me

"She expresses a most eager desire of being acquainted with me." [3]
Lady Susan, Chapter 3, Mrs. Vernon to Lady De Courcy.

I wish she had never come here

"How sincerely do I grieve that she ever entered this house!" [3]
Lady Susan, Chapter 11, Mrs. Vernon to Lady De Courcy

I can't stand the sight of her

"I have not yet tranquillised myself enough to see …" her. [3]
Lady Susan, Chapter 22, Lady Susan to Mrs. Johnson

I'll see you there

"…I shall there be rewarded by your society…"[3]
Lady Susan, Chapter 25, Lady Susan to Mrs. Johnson

It was great to see him

"I will not dissemble what real pleasure his sight afforded me…"[3]
Lady Susan, Chapter 29, Lady Susan Vernon to Mrs. Johnson

I have to postpone

"I yet feel myself under the necessity of delaying that hour beyond the time originally fixed." [3]
Lady Susan, Chapter 30, Lady Susan Vernon to Mr. De Courcy

Please visit us

"…it is our particular wish and entreaty that you would come to us as soon as you can." [3]
Lady Susan, Chapter 40, Lady De Courcy to Mrs. Vernon

He's fun to hang out with

"... the company of so good & so clever a Man ought to be gratifying in itself..."[2]
Jane Austen in a letter to Cassandra, Monday, February 9, 1807, about James

I hope she can come

"... the opportunity of her being conveyed hither will be excellent."[2]
Jane Austen in a letter to Cassandra, Friday, may 31, 1811, about Miss Sharp's visit

She was invited

"Her visits ... were continued by solicitation."[5]
Mansfield Park, Chapter 22, Narrator on Fanny's visits to the Parsonage

We agreed to hang out

We have entered into a contract of mutual agreeableness for the space of an evening, and all our agreeableness belongs solely to each other for that time."[6]
Northanger Abbey, Chapter 10, Mr. Tilney to Catherine about their dances together

They were always together

They "...hardly ever spent an evening asunder..."[7]
Persuasion, Chapter 6, Narrator on Anne & Mary

She liked hanging out with him

"His society became gradually her most exquisite enjoyment."[9]
Sense and Sensibility, Volume the First, Chapter 10, Narrator on Marianne with Willoughby

Separation

I hate good-byes

"Of all horrid things leave-taking is the worst."[1]
Emma, Chapter 30, Frank to Emma before leaving for Enscombe

He should be leaving any second now

I am "... in momentary expectation of his departure."[3]
Lady Susan, Chapter 24, Mrs. Vernon to Lady De Courcy

I've gotta bolt

"I have no time to spare, and therefore must now be gone directly."[1]
Emma, Chapter 45, Mr. Knightley to Emma about his leaving for London

"... it has been much against my inclination that we have stayed here so long."[10]
Edgar and Emma, Chapter 1, Lady Marlow to Sir Godfrey

My friends don't want me to leave

"My kind friends here are most affectionately urgent with me to prolong my stay."[3]
Lady Susan, Chapter 1, Lady Susan Vernon to Mr. Vernon.

Don't leave because of me

"I feel it my duty to entreat that you will not on my account shorten your visit here even an hour."[3]
Lady Susan, Chapter 25, Lady Susan to Mrs. Johnson

Either you go or I go

"...after what has passed between us it would ill suit the feelings of either to remain longer in the same house..."[3]
Lady Susan, Chapter 25, Lady Susan to Mrs. Johnson

We'll miss them

"We shall feel the loss of these two most agreeable young men exceedingly..."[2]
Jane Austen in a letter to Cassandra, Saturday, January 9, 1796, about Warren & Henry

I don't want her to leave

"I cannot say that I am in any hurry for the conclusion of her present visit."[2]
Jane Austen in a letter to Cassandra, Tuesday, December 28, 1808, about Mrs. Hookey

We wanted to be alone

"We were in hopes of being independant of other companions..."[2]
Jane Austen in a letter to Cassandra, Tuesday, January 17, 1809, about the coming assembly

She wants to leave home

"... she will be glad enough to be driven from her present wretched abode..."[2]
Jane Austen in a letter to Martha Lloyd, Tuesday, February 16, 1813, about Miss Benn

She would have missed him

"... how impossible it would have been for her to bear a lengthened absence."[5]
Mansfield Park, Chapter 19, Narrator on Lady Bertram upon Sir Thomas' return

She missed them

She "... thought of them ... with a degree of affectionate regret..."[5]
Mansfield Park, Chapter 21, Narrator on Fanny's thought of Maria & Julia after Maria's wedding

You will miss them

Their remoteness ... will be drawing forth bitter lamentations."[5]

Mansfield Park, Chapter 22, Mrs. Grant to Mary Crawford about the Mansfield servants

She wanted him to leave

"She could not compliment the ... gentleman ... with any appearance of interest in a scheme for extending his stay..."[5]

Mansfield Park, Chapter 23, Narrator on Fanny when Henry Crawford returned from Bath

We'll have fun without them

"... the absence of some is not to debar the others of amusement."[5]

Mansfield Park, Chapter 26, Sir Thomas to Mrs. Norris about holding a ball without Maria & Julia

I miss you

"I have been quite wretched without you."[6]

Northanger Abbey, Chapter 8, Isabella to Catherine after being separated

She said a sad good-bye

"... with ... most exquisite misery, and ... utter despondency, she bade her friend adieu..."[6]

Northanger Abbey, Chapter 9, Narrator on Isabella leaving Catherine after the carriage rides

He couldn't charm her into staying

"It was not in the power of all his gallantry to detain her longer."[6]

Northanger Abbey, Chapter 15, Narrator on John Thorpe hinting marriage to Catherine

She wanted to leave

"... her inclination was growing strong for a removal..."[7]

Persuasion, Chapter 3, Narrator on Elizabeth

"... she was wildly urgent to be gone."[9]

Sense and Sensibility, Volume the Second, Chapter 9, Narrator on Marianne wanting to go home

I need to be alone right now

I require "... a long application of solitude and reflection to recover..."[7]

Persuasion, Chapter 9, Narrator on Anne being assisted by Wentworth

She needed more time to calm down

"Half an hour's solitude and reflection might have tranquillised her..."[7]

Persuasion, Chapter 23, Narrator on Anne's reaction to Wentworth's letter

Good riddance

"The moment of her release from him was ecstasy."[8]

Pride and Prejudice, Chapter 18, Narrator on Elizabeth finishing her two dances with Mr. Collins

They grew apart

"... all the comfort of intimacy was over..."[8]

Pride and Prejudice, Chapter 26, Narrator on Elizabeth & Charlotte after Charlotte's wedding

He had to say good-bye

"... he took the opportunity of paying the parting civilities which he deemed indispensably necessary."[8]

Pride and Prejudice, Chapter 38, Narrator on Mr. Collins as Elizabeth departed Hunsford

She wanted to avoid him

"… any meeting with him would have been the last object of her wishes."[8]
Pride and Prejudice, Chapter 50, Narrator on Elizabeth seeing Mr. Wickham after his wedding

She was missing him

"… she courted the misery which a contrast between the past and present was certain of giving."[9]
Sense and Sensibility, Volume the First, Chapter 16, Narrator on Marianne missing Willoughby

They needed some time apart

She "… began to foresee … a variety of advantages that would accrue to them … from this separation."[9]
Sense and Sensibility, Volume the Second, Chapter 3, Narrator on Mrs. Dashwood approving the trip to London

They avoided each other

"Design could never bring them in each other's way…"[9]
Sense and Sensibility, Volume the Second, Chapter 10, Narrator on Marianne & Willoughby in London

Spending Time

He killed some time

"...he found occupation for an idle hour..."[7]
Persuasion, Chapter 1, Narrator on Sir Walter Elliot

There was too much going on

"Every moment rather brought fresh agitation."[7]
Persuasion, Chapter 23, Narrator on Anne's reaction to Wentworth's letter

It's hard to find quality time

"... it is impossible that every moment should be employed in conversing together."[8]
Pride and Prejudice, Chapter 6, Charlotte to Elizabeth on Jane & Mr. Bingley

Don't do more than you have to

"... exertion should always be in proportion to what is required."[8]
Pride and Prejudice, Chapter 7, Mary to Elizabeth on Elizabeth walking to Netherfield

Content to watch

"... sufficiently amused in attending to what passed..."[8]
Pride and Prejudice, Chapter 10, Narrator on Elizabeth watching Mr. Darcy & Miss Bingley

Their normal routine

"... the quiet tenor of their usual employments..."[8]
Pride and Prejudice, Chapter 28, Narrator on Elizabeth's musings at Hunsford

She decided to take a walk

"… she resolved … to indulge herself in air and exercise."[8]
Pride and Prejudice, Chapter 35, Narrator on Elizabeth's condition after Mr. Darcy's proposal

You had a good time

"… your … visit cannot have been entirely irksome."[8]
Pride and Prejudice, Chapter 38, Mr. Collins to Elizabeth about her stay at Hunsford

It would be a great idea

"It would be such a delicious scheme…"[8]
Pride and Prejudice, Chapter 39, Lydia to Elizabeth & Jane about going to Brighton

To go about their day

"… to pursue the usual course of their employments."[8]
Pride and Prejudice, Chapter 41, Narrator on Jane & Elizabeth after the regiment left Meryton

They went out

"… the schemes of amusement … abroad … were put in execution."[9]
Sense and Sensibility, Volume the First, Chapter 11, Narrator on Sir John's plans

Just because it's fun doesn't make it a good idea

"… the pleasantness of an employment does not always evince its propriety."[9]
Sense and Sensibility, Volume the First, Chapter 13, Elinor to Marianne about going with Willoughby to Allenham

The wait was over

"... her mind was no longer supported by the fever of suspense..."[9]

Sense and Sensibility, Volume the Second, Chapter 7, Narrator on Marianne after Willoughby's letter

She's wasting her time

"... she has ... given up a great deal of time to no purpose..."[3]

The Watsons, Elizabeth to Emma about Penelope's attempts to attach Dr. Harding

A fun time

"... the happy occupation..."[3]

The Watsons, Narrator on Emma getting dressed for the assembly

To study

"... to be laboring to enlarge her comprehension or exercise it on sober facts..."[1]

Emma, Chapter 9, Narrator on Harriet & Emma not fulfilling their academic goals

Going to work

"... enjoyments of ease and leisure ... must now be relinquished."[1]

Emma, Chapter 20, Narrator on Jane beginning her career as a teacher

She's starting a new job

She is "... beginning her career of laborious duty."[1]

Emma, Chapter 20, Narrator on Jane beginning her career as a teacher

I had time to think about us

"...I had ample leisure for reflection on the present state of our affairs..."[3]

Lady Susan, Chapter 30, Lady Susan Vernon to Mr. De Courcy

It was very entertaining

It "... has diverted me beyond moderation."[2]
Jane Austen in a letter to Cassandra, Thursday, September 1, 1796,
about a letter she received from Cassandra

It was slow going

It "... was not quite so expeditiously
performed..."[2]
Jane Austen in a letter to Cassandra, Wednesday, October 24, 1798,
about one stage of a road trip

They keep you busy

"... they force one into constant exertion."[2]
Jane Austen in a letter to Cassandra, Thursday, May 21, 1801, about
tiny parties

We had fun too

"Our evening was equally agreeable in its
way..."[2]
Jane Austen in a letter to Cassandra, Monday, October 24, 1808, about
the games after the water party

We had a good day

"... with us it was a Prince of days..."[2]
Jane Austen in a letter to Cassandra, Sunday, November 20, 1808, about
the weather the previous Thursday

What a waste of my time

"Unlucky, that I should have wasted so much
reflection on the subject!"[2]
Jane Austen in a letter to Cassandra, Tuesday, January 10, 1809, about
the St. Albans leaving Portsmouth

You'll keep busy

"I can easily suppose that your ... weeks here
will be fully occupied..."[2]
Jane Austen in a letter to Cassandra, Tuesday, January 17, 1809, about
Cassandra's visit

We don't have much going on right now

"... it seems a more disengaged period with us, than we are likely to have later..."[2]
Jane Austen in a letter to Cassandra, Friday, may 31, 1811, about the early summer

It entertained me

"It diverted me exceedingly."[2]
Jane Austen in a letter to Cassandra, Wednesday, March 2, 1814, about reading *The Heroine*, by Eaton Stannard Barrett[2]

I've been busy

"... I can command very little quiet time at present..."[2]
Jane Austen in a letter to Fanny Knight, Friday, November 18, 1814, excusing her inability to write

Real quickly

"... involving the smallest tax on your time."[2]
Jane Austen in a letter to John Murray, Monday, December 11, 1815, about settling the publication details for *Emma*

Don't wear yourself out too much

"This will be a bad day's amusement for you if you are to be knocked up."[5]
Mansfield Park, Chapter 9, Edmund to Fanny during the walk around Sotherton

They had sort of a bummer trip

"... their ramble did not appear to have been more than partially agreeable..."[5]
Mansfield Park, Chapter 10, Narrator on Maria, Mr. Rushworth, & Henry Crawford upon their return to the Sotherton house

He had never tried it

"... in all the riot of his gratifications, it was yet an untasted pleasure..."[5]
Mansfield Park, Chapter 13, Narrator on Henry Crawford acting in a play

Busy

"... being engaged apart in some manner of business ... which seemed entirely to engross..."[5]
Mansfield Park, Chapter 23, Narrator on Edmund in conversation with Dr. Grant

Take your time

"Do not hurry yourself, I entreat."[5]
Mansfield Park, Chapter 31, Henry Crawford to Fanny about the letter she wrote to Mary Crawford

He was easily entertained

"Everything supplied an amusement to the high glee of ... mind..."[5]
Mansfield Park, Chapter 38, Narrator on Fanny & William on the trip to Portsmouth

She appreciated down time

She "... learned to think it no misfortune to be quietly employed."[5]
Mansfield Park, Chapter 40, Narrator on Susan after Fanny's influence

To waste time

"... to leave them little leisure for serious employment."[9]
Sense and Sensibility, Volume the First, Chapter 11, Narrator on the Dashwoods' many visitors

She had to wait

"... it was not immediately that an opportunity ... could be commanded..."[9]
Sense and Sensibility, Volume the Second, Chapter 1, Narrator on Elinor talking to Lucy Steele

She couldn't make up her mind

She "... dawdled away her time in rapture and indecision."9

Sense and Sensibility, Volume the Second, Chapter 4, Narrator on Mrs. Palmer in the London shops

She had a tough night

"... the evening was by no means ... productive of pleasure to her..."9

Sense and Sensibility, Volume the Second, Chapter 4, Narrator on Marianne the 2nd night in London

Get a quick look at the picture

"... to take more expeditiously the dimensions of a print..."9

Sense and Sensibility, Volume the Third, Chapter 3, Narrator on Elinor moving to the window

That wasn't all they thought about

"The whole of their mental vivacity was evidently not so employed..."3

Sanditon, Chapter 10, Narrator on Mr. Parker's siblings and their physical complaints

They slowed down to take a look

"... there could be no possibility of the two friends passing it without a slackened pace and observing eyes."1

Emma, Chapter 10, Narrator on Emma & Harriet passing the vicarage

They worked their way through the crowd

"... by a continued exertion of strength and ingenuity they found themselves at last in the passage..."6

Northanger Abbey, Chapter 2, Narrator on Catherine & Mrs. Allen in the crowds at Bath

Nobody interrupted their plans

They had "... no impertinent intrusion to disconcert their measures..."[6]
Northanger Abbey, Chapter 14, Narrator on Catherine's walk with the Tilneys

Staying up way too late

"... so serious a delay of proper repose."[6]
Northanger Abbey, Chapter 23, Narrator on General Tilney

She was active

Her "... disposition was not naturally sedentary..."[6]
Northanger Abbey, Chapter 30, Narrator on Catherine

"... with a disposition much less inclined to sedentary pursuits..."[5]
Mansfield Park, Chapter 43, Narrator on Susan

Luck/Fortune & Misfortune

My bad luck

"... the combination of misfortunes under which I laboured..."[10]

Love and Friendship, Letter 6th, Laura quoting Edward to Marianne

She was so lucky

She "...seemed to unite some of the best blessings of existence..."[1]

Emma, Chapter 1, Narrator's description of Emma Woodhouse

He's unlucky

"He is quite the Dregs of the family as to Luck."[2]

Jane Austen in a letter to Cassandra, Tuesday, October 26, 1813, about Edward Bridges

It was meant to be

"... it seems to have been the merciful appointment of Providence..."[5]

Mansfield Park, Chapter 47, Edmund to Fanny on her not being hurt by Henry Crawford

It was a tough break

"... the change was such as might have plunged weak spirits in despondence."[3]

The Watsons, Narrator on the changes in Emma's circumstances

Money Matters

We should have given her money

"It was proper to render her pecuniary assistance." [3]

Lady Susan, Chapter 3, Mrs. Vernon to Lady De Courcy

Amateur (not professionally)

"... without any view to pecuniary Emolument." [2]

Jane Austen in a letter to Cassandra, Thursday January 14, 1796, about why she writes

It was cheap

"... the sum was so trifling..." [2]

Jane Austen in a letter to Cassandra, Thursday, May 21, 1801, about a box of lozenges

She did not have many expenses

"... there was nothing to impede her frugality..." [5]

Mansfield Park, Chapter 1, Narrator on Mrs. Norris

Its financial importance

"The necessity of the measure in a pecuniary light..." [5]

Mansfield Park, Chapter 3, Narrator on Sir Thomas's voyage to Antigua

To hell with the cost

"The expense need not be any impediment." [5]

Mansfield Park, Chapter 6, Mrs. Norris to Mr. Rushworth about the improvements to his estate

Their poverty

"... their pecuniary distress..." [10]

Love and Friendship, Letter 9th, Laura to Marianne about Augustus & Sophia

Homeless

"... unprovided with any habitation..."[10]

Love and Friendship, Letter 10th, Laura to Marianne about Edward's disappearance

Dirt poor

"... every pecuniary Distress that Poverty could inflict..."[4]

Lesley Castle, Margaret to Charlotte on Louisa before marrying

She thought they should quickly pay their debts by any means

"She considered it as an act of indispensable duty to clear away the claims of creditors with all the expedition which the most comprehensive retrenchments could secure..."[7]

Persuasion, Chapter 2, Narrator on Anne

To make it through tough times

To face "... a trial of fortitude which stronger heads ... have found too much."[7]

Persuasion, Chapter 2, Narrator on Sir Walter

To be filthy rich

To have "... nothing to wish for on the side of avarice or indulgence..."[7]

Persuasion, Chapter 21, Mrs. Smith on Mr. Elliot's wealth

Paid her back

"... fully requited the services which she had rendered..."[7]

Persuasion, Chapter 24, Narrator on Wentworth securing Mrs. Smith's property

She could live on less

"... a much smaller provision ... would support her in affluence."[9]
Sense and Sensibility, Volume the First, Chapter 3, Narrator on Mrs. Dashwood

He would have been poor

"He would then have suffered under the pecuniary distresses..."[9]
Sense and Sensibility, Volume the Third, Chapter 11, Elinor to Marianne about Willoughby

Poverty

"... pecuniary difficulties..."[3]
Sanditon, Chapter 3, Narrator on the Breretons

He can't afford it

"... the expense alas! ... was ill-suited to his purse..."[3]
Sanditon, Chapter 8, Narrator on Sir Edward buying a house for Clara

Sadness

Depression

She had sad thoughts

She "... resumed a more serious, more dispiriting cogitation..."[1]

Emma, Chapter 16, Narrator on Emma thinking about telling Harriet about Mr. Elton

They were upset

They "... were both dreadfully desponding."[1]

Emma, Chapter 36, Mr. Weston to Mrs. Elton about Mrs. Weston & Frank

She felt sad

"She was vexed beyond what could have been expressed..."[1]

Emma, Chapter 43, Narrator on Emma after being confronted by Mr. Knightley

"... she had to struggle against a great tendency to lowness."[7]

Persuasion, Chapter 11, Narrator on Anne meeting Wentworth's friends

"...the despondence that sunk her little heart was severe."[5]

Mansfield Park, Chapter 2, Narrator on Fanny when she first came to Mansfield Park

"...the happy spirits which had seldom been depressed before, were now so much affected as to make it almost impossible for her to appear tolerably cheerful."[8]

Pride and Prejudice, Chapter 37, Narrator on Elizabeth considering what Jane had lost

"It was some time, however, before a smile could be extorted from..."[8]her.
Pride and Prejudice, Chapter 40, Narrator on Jane's reaction to the report of Mr. Wickham's character

She sounded sad

"There was not the same cheerful volubility..."[1]
Emma, Chapter 44, Narrator on Emma's visit to Miss Bates after Box Hill

We were sad

"Everybody had a degree of gravity and sorrow..."[1]
Emma, Chapter 45, Narrator on Mrs. Churchill's death

She complained

"... her heart was too full to contain its afflictions."[10]
Edgar and Emma, Chapter 2, Narrator on Emma when Edgar did not come with the Willmots

Her sadness

"... the melancholy disappointment under which she laboured."[10]
Edgar and Emma, Chapter 2, Narrator on Emma when Edgar did not come with the Willmots

She kept crying

"... having no check to the overflowings of her grief, she gave free vent to them, and ... continued in tears..."[10]
Edgar and Emma, Chapter 3, Narrator on Emma finding out that Edgar is at college

She seemed turned off

"A soft languor spread over her lovely features..."[10]
Love and Friendship, Letter 8th, Laura to Marianne about Sophia

I miss my friends

"... there is nothing so bad as parting with one's friends. One seems so forlorn without them."[8]
Pride and Prejudice, Chapter 53, Mrs. Bennet to Elizabeth on Lydia's marriage & departure

It was very upsetting

"The discomposure of spirits ... could not be easily overcome..."[8]
Pride and Prejudice, Chapter 57, Narrator on Elizabeth after the visit from Lady Catherine

He was naturally sad

He "... was not of a disposition in which happiness overflows in mirth..."[8]
Pride and Prejudice, Chapter 59, Narrator on Mr. Darcy at the dinner table after his engagement to Elizabeth

Life sucks

"Such is the depravity of the world!"[10]
Love and Friendship, Letter 10th, Laura to Marianne after Augusts' arrest & Edward's disappearance

She was really upset

She "... was more violent than ever in her lamentations..."[10]
Catherine, Narrator on Camilla about Catherine missing the ball

"... her grief and agitation were excessive."[6]
Northanger Abbey, Chapter 29, Narrator on Catherine passing Woodston on her way home

Man, I was so happy, and then it all went to hell

"Little did I imagine ... that the delightful perturbation of spirits I was then in would undergo so speedy, so melancholy a reverse."[3]
Lady Susan, Chapter 24, Mrs. Vernon to Lady De Courcy

That's gotta suck

It "… must be a very severe affliction…"[2]
Jane Austen in a letter to Philadelphia Walter, Sunday, April 8, 1798, about the death of his father

Things have kinda sucked lately

"We have been in two or three dreadful states within the last week…"[2]
Jane Austen in a letter to Cassandra, Tuesday, January 24, 1809, about the melting snows

She was sickened by sadness

"The state of her spirits had probably had its share in her indisposition…"[5]
Mansfield Park, Chapter 7, Narrator on Fanny's reaction to Edmund & Mary Crawford monopolizing Fanny's horse

Laugh now … cry later

"A few moments of feverish enjoyment were followed by hours of acute suffering."[5]
Mansfield Park, Chapter 20, Narrator on Maria when Henry Crawford announced his leaving for Bath

She had painful thoughts

"… the agony of her mind was severe."[5]
Mansfield Park, Chapter 20, Narrator on Maria when Henry Crawford announced his leaving for Bath

"These convictions must unquestionably have their own pain…"[7]
Persuasion, Chapter 13, Narrator on Anne's realization that the Crofts were better suited to Kellynch than the Elliots

Bothered

"… in the utmost perturbation and dismay."[5]
Mansfield Park, Chapter 32, Narrator on Fanny listening to Sir Thomas' lecture

He looked shaken

"... the disturbance of his mind was visible in every feature."[8]
Pride and Prejudice, Chapter 34, Narrator on Mr. Darcy's reaction to Elizabeth's reply to his proposal

It's been rough

"... I have never known the blessing of one tranquil hour..."[1]
Emma, Chapter 48, Mrs. Weston to Emma, quoting Jane

That didn't make her feel any better

"... there was nothing in that to soothe irritation..."[5]
Mansfield Park, Chapter 44, Narrator on Fanny considering Edmunds letter

I'm sad

"My present state is miserably irksome."[5]
Mansfield Park, Chapter 44, Edmund in a letter to Fanny

"...I am excessively vexed..."[3]
Lady Susan, Chapter 13, Lady De Courcy to Mrs. Vernon

She must hate life

"What can exceed the misery of such a mind in such a situation?"[5]
Mansfield Park, Chapter 48, Narrator on Maria after her break from Henry Crawford

I wouldn't have liked that

"... that would have thrown me into agonies!"[6]
Northanger Abbey, Chapter 6, Isabella to Catherine about the rainy weather

It made her sad

It "... affected her spirits exceedingly..."[7]
Persuasion, Chapter 6, Narrator on Mrs. Musgrove

"... she bewailed it as exceedingly unlucky..."[8]
Pride and Prejudice, Chapter 21, Narrator on Mrs. Bennet's reaction to Mr. Bingley leaving Netherfield

"... her happiness would have a material drawback..."[5]
Mansfield Park, Chapter 43, Narrator on Fanny leaving Susan behind

The blues

"... occasional effusions of sorrow..."[9]
Sense and Sensibility, Volume the First, Chapter 16, Narrator on Marianne missing Willoughby

Her bawling

"... this torrent of unresisted grief..."[9]
Sense and Sensibility, Volume the Second, Chapter 7, Narrator on Marianne after Willoughby's letter

To be negative

To allow "... the admission of every melancholy idea..."[9]
Sense and Sensibility, Volume the Third, Chapter 7, Narrator on Col. Brandon and Marianne's illness

Regret & Guilt

She felt ashamed

It "... made her think that she should never be in charity with herself again."[1]
Emma, Chapter 17, Narrator on Emma telling Harriet about Mr. Elton

"... she felt it with all the pain of continual self-reproach..."[9]
Sense and Sensibility, Volume the Third, Chapter 2, Narrator on Marianne considering Elinor's hidden pain

She gave in but regretted it

"... the forbearance of her outward submission left a heavy arrear due of secret severity..."[1]
Emma, Chapter 42, Narrator on Emma agreeing to be part of Mrs. Elton's party to Box Hill

Her mistakes

"The blunders, the blindness of her own head and heart!"[1]
Emma, Chapter 47, Narrator on Emma's thought of herself after being convinced of Mr. Knightley's admiration of Harriet

To my regret

"...to my great vexation..."[3]
Lady Susan, Chapter 13, Lady De Courcy to Mrs. Vernon

I regret it

"The consequence ... has been a state of perpetual suffering to me..."[1]
Emma, Chapter 48, Mrs. Weston to Emma, quoting Jane

"It is, in fact, a most mortifying retrospect for me."[1]
Emma, Chapter 50, Frank in a letter to Mrs. Weston, about his behavior in Highbury

It "... awakened all my remorse."[9]
Sense and Sensibility, Volume the Third, Chapter 8, Willoughby to Elinor about Marianne's letters

She regretted

"Fixed there by the keenest of all anguish, self reproach, she could find no interval of ease or forgetfulness."[8]
Pride and Prejudice, Chapter 47, Narrator on Elizabeth's thoughts during the ride back to Longbourn

"The consciousness of having done amiss had exposed her to a thousand inquietudes..."[1]
Emma, Chapter 48, Mrs. Weston to Emma on Jane's guilt

"... the reflection of her past folly operated so strongly on her mind..."[10]
Frederic and Elfrida, Chapter 4, Narrator on Charlotte after her double engagement

"In her own past behavior, there was a constant source of vexation..."[8]
Pride and Prejudice, Chapter 37, Narrator on Elizabeth's recollections of her treatment of Mr. Darcy

Sometimes she felt guilty

"... there were moments of self-examination in which her conscience could not quite acquit her."[1]
Emma, Chapter 20, Narrator on Emma's reasons for not liking Jane

He must feel guilty

"How unpleasant, one would think, must be his reflections!"[3]
Lady Susan, Chapter 22, Lady Susan to Mrs. Johnson

"... his conscience reproaches him..."[2]
Jane Austen in a letter to Cassandra, Thursday, November 20, 1800, referring to Charles & Miss Terry

It "... left him with the stings of conscience."[6]
Northanger Abbey, Chapter 23, Narrator on General Tilney and Mrs. Tilney's room

Giving her a guilt trip

"... being able to bring her to any proper sense of Shame-"[2]
Jane Austen in a letter to Cassandra, Thursday, September 15, 1796, about Miss Fletcher's negligence in writing

They apologized

"… they breathed a strong spirit of regret…"[2]

Jane Austen in a letter to Miss Bigg, Friday, January 24, 1817, about Alethea's letters from abroad

They all felt guilty

"… every … heart was sinking under some degree of self-condemnation…"[5]

Mansfield Park, Chapter 19, Narrator on the mood of the house when Sir Thomas returned

She felt low

"She felt humble to the dust."[6]

Northanger Abbey, Chapter 22, Narrator on Catherine after reading the laundry bill

Regretting it

"… bitterly lamenting that it had ever been thought of…"[7]

Persuasion, Chapter 12, Narrator on Henrietta

Regretting his behavior

"… lamenting the blindness of his own pride, and the blunders of his own calculations…"[7]

Persuasion, Chapter 23, Narrator on Wentworth

Gees, you must feel rotten about it

"… mortifying and humiliating must be the origin of those regrets…"[9]

Sense and Sensibility, Volume the Second, Chapter 10, Narrator on Mrs. Dashwood's letters to Marianne

There's no point dwelling on it now

"… it brought only the torture of penitence, without the hope of amendment."[9]

Sense and Sensibility, Volume the Third, Chapter 2, Narrator on Marianne considering Elinor's hidden pain

I feel guilty

"I owe such a grudge to myself for the stupid, rascally folly of my own heart..."[9]

Sense and Sensibility, Volume the Third, Chapter 8, Willoughby to Elinor explaining his behavior

I'm such a jerk

"I cannot express my own abhorrence of myself."[9]

Sense and Sensibility, Volume the Third, Chapter 10, Marianne to Elinor

She really wished she were better

"She did unfeignedly and unequivocally regret the inferiority..."[1]

Emma, Chapter 27, Narrator on Emma comparing her playing & singing to Jane's

I shouldn't have taken your side

"...I should not have espoused your cause..."[3]

Lady Susan, Chapter 24, Mrs. Vernon to Lady De Courcy

Seize the day

"How often is happiness destroyed by preparation, foolish preparation?"[1]

Emma, Chapter 30, Frank to Emma about putting off the ball

I paid for my mistakes

"... what a state my imprudence reduced me to..."[2]

Jane Austen in a letter to Cassandra, Tuesday, June 11, 1799, about buying a cheap muslin veil

She's only sorry she got caught

"... it was the detection, not the offense, which she reprobated."[5]

Mansfield Park, Chapter 47, Edmund to Fanny on Mary Crawford's view of the scandal

He screwed up big time

"… his mistakes could sometimes be very egregious."[6]
Northanger Abbey, Chapter 18, Narrator on John Thorpe

Loneliness

On my own

"… destitute of any support…"[10]
Love and Friendship, Letter 10th, Laura to Marianne about Edward's disappearance

I was sad and lonely

"Now it was languor, and all but solitude."[5]
Mansfield Park, Chapter 29, Narrator on Fanny being alone with Lady Bertram after the ball

She was lonely

"She could not live any longer in such solitary wretchedness…"[5]
Mansfield Park, Chapter 29, Narrator on May Crawford after Edmund left

Being different sucks

"… it is singularity which often makes the worst part of our suffering…"[7]
Persuasion, Chapter 2, Lady Russell to Anne

She hated being alone

"She had no resources for solitude…"[7]
Persuasion, Chapter 5, Narrator on Mary

Being ignored is a bummer

"To be neglected before one's time must be very vexatious…"[5]
Mansfield Park, Chapter 5, Mary Crawford to Thomas Bertram

Embarrassment

It would have embarrassed him

He "...could not have borne the degradation..."[7]
Persuasion, Chapter 2, Narrator on Sir Walter lowering his expenses

She got embarrassed

"A fine blush ... succeeded the previous paleness of her face."[5]
Mansfield Park, Chapter 19, Narrator on Fanny when Sir Thomas complimented her appearance

Dislike & Hardship

I would hate them

"How odious I should think them!"[8]
Pride and Prejudice, Chapter 10, Caroline Bingley to Mr. Darcy on writing business letters

We had a lot of cr*p to deal with

"... scenes of great agitation awaited us, and there was much to be endured..."[2]
Jane Austen in a letter to Cassandra, Tuesday, August 27, 1805, about the trip to Goodnestone Farm

He didn't like it as much

His "... gratification was less keen..."[2]
Jane Austen in a letter to Frank, Saturday, September 25, 1813, comparing Henry & his son Edward's appreciation of nature

She couldn't hold herself together

"I did not use to think her wanting in self-possession, but she had not quite enough for the demands of yesterday."[5]
Mansfield Park, Chapter 40, Mary Crawford in a letter to Fanny about Maria

It'll be awkward for you

"...you will be uncomfortably circumstanced."[6]

Northanger Abbey, Chapter 25, James in a letter to Catherine about Captain Tilney's return to Northanger Abbey

Surprise & Knowing

She was shocked

It "... struck so forcibly on her mind, that she could hardly restrain her astonishment from being visible."[8]
Pride and Prejudice, Chapter 44, Narrator on Elizabeth's notice of the change in Mr. Darcy's manners

"...her chief profit was in wonder."[6]
Northanger Abbey, Chapter 18, Narrator on Catherine considering John Thorpe's presumed understanding

"...her astonishment was consequently so great as to overcome at first the bounds of decorum..."[8]
Pride and Prejudice, Chapter 22, Narrator on Elizabeth's reaction to Charlotte's engagement to Mr. Collins

She had "...feelings which had kept her face averted and her tongue motionless."[1]
Emma, Chapter 43, Narrator on Emma's embarrassment after being confronted by Mr. Knightley

She "...was still overpowered by the suddenness...so wholly unexpected, and the novelty of a situation which her fancy had never taken into account."[5]
Mansfield Park, Chapter 33, Narrator on what Henry Crawford imagined to be the reason for Fanny's refusal

It was surprising

It "...was a matter of lively astonishment."[6]
Northanger Abbey, Chapter 18, Narrator on Catherine considering John Thorpe's attachment

It "...was a circumstance to raise no common degree of astonishment."[6]
Northanger Abbey, Chapter 21, Narrator on the chest in Catherine's room

"I am all astonishment."[8]
Pride and Prejudice, Chapter 6, Caroline Bingley to Mr. Darcy on his attraction to Elizabeth

It was "...of a different nature than anything foreboded..."[1]
Emma, Chapter 45, Narrator on the cause of Mrs. Churchill's death

We were surprised

"It came upon us without much preparation..."[2]
Jane Austen in a letter to Frank, Saturday, September 25, 1813, about Anna's engagement to Ben Lefroy

We couldn't stop staring

"... every thought was now engaged by the horrid spectacle before us."[10]
Love and Friendship, Letter 13th, Laura to Marianne about the phaeton crash with Edward & Augustus

That sure popped up fast

"I was very far from expecting so speedy a distinction." [3]
Lady Susan, Chapter 3, Mrs. Vernon to Lady De Courcy.

He seemed shocked

"...he appeared all astonishment and perplexity..."[3]
Lady Susan, Chapter 20, Mrs. Vernon to Lady De Courcy

I can't even guess

"I am bewildered in my endeavours to form some rational conjecture..."[3]
Lady Susan, Chapter 35, Lady Susan to Mr. De Courcy

I know

"...I am fortunately enabled absolutely to ascertain."[2]

Jane Austen in a letter to Cassandra, Monday, November 30, 1800, referring to the time by the Shewsbury Clock

I should have seen it coming

"I was foolish not to provide better against such a Possibility."[2]

Jane Austen in a letter to Cassandra, Thursday, March 3, 1814, about her trunk not arriving on time

I'm surprised

"...my strongest sensation of all is astonishment..."[2]

Jane Austen in a letter to Fanny Knight, Sunday, March 23, 1817, about Fanny's conversation with Mr. Wildman

It was worse than she could have imagined

"She could not have supposed it in the power of any concurrence of circumstances to give her so many painful sensations..."[5]

Mansfield Park, Chapter 31, Narrator on Fanny anticipating Henry Crawford's return for dinner

A strange thing

"...one of the most extraordinary and unaccountable circumstances..."[9]

Sense and Sensibility, Volume the Third, Chapter 13, Narrator on Lucy's marriage to Robert Ferrars

Lots of them

"...more than I can enumerate."[1]

Emma, Chapter 32, Mrs. Elton to Emma about friends who had given up music

Quietly

"...with no sullen sound that could alarm a human being."[6]

Northanger Abbey, Chapter 24, Narrator on Catherine entering Mrs. Tilney's room

Remembrance & Forgetting

Remembrance

It brings back memories

"...to raise the violent emotion which it produced for a while..."[9]

Sense and Sensibility, Volume the First, Chapter 3, Narrator on Mrs. Dashwood remaining at Norland

She thought about him

"...so fervently did she value his remembrance..."[8]

Pride and Prejudice, Chapter 40, Narrator on Jane's thoughts of Mr. Bingley

His ability to hold a grudge

"...the implacability of his resentments..."[8]

Pride and Prejudice, Chapter 16, Elizabeth to Mr. Wickham about Mr. Darcy

You sure hold a grudge

"...your resentment once created was unappeasable."[8]

Pride and Prejudice, Chapter 18, Elizabeth to Mr. Darcy

She stayed up late thinking about it

She "... awoke the next morning to the same thoughts and meditations which had at length closed her eyes."[8]

Pride and Prejudice, Chapter 35, Narrator on Elizabeth thinking about Mr. Darcy's proposal

A pleasant memory

"... a recollection ... not untinctured by tenderness..."[8]
Pride and Prejudice, Chapter 44, Narrator on Mr. Bingley's memories of Jane

Dwelling on the past

"... heightening ... affliction by melancholy remembrances..."[9]
Sense and Sensibility, Volume the First, Chapter 3, Narrator on Mrs. Dashwood

Bad memories

"... bringing back the past in the strongest and most afflicting manner..."[9]
Sense and Sensibility, Volume the Second, Chapter 10, Narrator on Marianne returning to Barton

A warm memory

"...a dearer, tenderer recollection."[1]
Emma, Chapter 1, Narrator – Emma missing Miss Taylor.

She died a long time ago

She "... has long paid the debt of nature."[10]
Love and Friendship, Letter 15th, Laura to Marianne about Philippa

He died

He "... has closed his virtuous & happy life..."[2]
Jane Austen in a letter to Frank, Monday, January 21, 1805, about their father's death

He built up good memories

"... he had secured agreeable recollections for his own mind."[5]
Mansfield Park, Chapter 41, Narrator on Henry Crawford's business in Norfolk

Forgetting

She tried not to dwell on it

"... all her good sense, and all her attention ... were requisite to check the indulgence of those regrets ..."[8]

Pride and Prejudice, Chapter 40, Narrator on Jane's thoughts of Mr. Bingley

She couldn't remember

"But no such recollection befriended her."[8]

Pride and Prejudice, Chapter 36, Narrator on Elizabeth trying to recall Mr. Wickham's behavior

It's better off forgotten

"But in such cases as these, a good memory is unpardonable."[8]

Pride and Prejudice, Chapter 59, Elizabeth to Jane, about the early opinions of Mr. Darcy

She hardly remembers her

She has no "...more than an indistinct remembrance of her ..."[1]

Emma, Chapter 1, Narrator's description of the Woodhouse family

Help him to forget

"... contribute to obliterate from his remembrance, those disagreable Events..."[4]

Lesley Castle, Charlotte to Margaret on Lesley traveling

It was a silly notion, so I forgot about it

"...this was too idle and nonsensical an idea to remain long on my mind..."[3]

Lady Susan, Chapter 29, Lady Susan Vernon to Mrs. Johnson

Time & Passage of Time

Two weeks from tomorrow

"Tomorrow fortnight."[8]

Pride and Prejudice, Chapter 2, Elizabeth on the public assembly

Time heals all wounds

"Such violence of affliction indeed could not be supported for ever..."[9]

Sense and Sensibility, Volume the First, Chapter 16, Narrator on Marianne missing Willoughby

All of a sudden

"... in a most abrupt and precipitate manner."[10]

Love and Friendship, Letter 13th, Laura to Marianne about Macdonald walking in on Sophia stealing

Middle-aged

"...too old to be agreeable, too young to die."[3]

Lady Susan, Chapter 29, Lady Susan Vernon to Mrs. Johnson

It comes and goes

"It will all go on exceedingly well, and decline away in a very reasonable manner."[2]

Jane Austen in a letter to Cassandra, Saturday, November 17, 1798, about people's attentions to Mrs. Austen

He'll eventually get over it

"Time would undoubtedly abate somewhat of his sufferings..."[5]

Mansfield Park, Chapter 47, Narrator on Edmund getting over Mary Crawford

What a long two weeks

"… a devilishly long fortnight it will appear to me."[6]

Northanger Abbey, Chapter 15, John Thorpe hinting marriage to Catherine

It was a long wait

"… many were the tedious hours which must yet intervene."[6]

Northanger Abbey, Chapter 21, Narrator on Catherine waiting until morning to read the found manuscript

The time dragged by

"… the short period that intervened … hung heavily on their hands, and every hour was too long."[10]

Catherine, Narrator on Catherine & Camilla waiting for the Dudleys' ball

Vividly Colorful and Moderately Sarcastic Glossary

Abatement (n) – The lessening of some extreme condition of being; the moderation of an extremity, often of an emotional state; the mitigation of a wretchedness.

Abhorrence (n) – A sensation of extreme disgust; a cosmic degree of hatred; a furious repugnance, inclining one to smash things or kick a puppy.

Ablution (n) – A cleansing or purification; a purging, often more ritualistic and ceremonious than practical, like showering after speaking on the phone with a filthy person, or like changing shirts after work just to throw off the "workness" of the other shirt.

Abominate (v) – To find utterly disgusting; to regard with teeth-grinding, skin-crawling hatred.

Acquiescence (n) – The act of caving to the will of another; the crumbling of one's spine, resulting in the abandonment of ideals and opinions.

Acrimony (n) – Sharp bitterness of thought or language; the cruel treatment of another; meanness, sharpness of tongue, or a blatant attack on the feelings of others.

Affability (n) – The state of being approachable or warmly welcoming, the kind of person people easily turn to.

Allay (v) – To subdue fussiness; to calm by the elimination of a demeanor irritant.

Approbation (n) – The state of liking, appreciating, digging; the consideration of something to be the bomb, aces, sick, wicked, or phat; the state of giving something or someone kudos or props.

Apropos (adj) – Coincidentally ideal; providentially bestowed; fittingly advantageous; the perfectly right thing at the perfectly right time; right on; on the mark.

Autumnal (adj) – Occurring in, or bearing a resemblance to, the season of autumn; possessing the colors, coolness, or sentiments associated with autumn; being in the latter quarter of existence, fading, inclining toward decay and death.

Avarice (n) – A desire for wealth or consequence, used usually to represent dubious desires of despicable characters in their unscrupulous and damaging quest for riches or consequence.

Caprice (n) – Abrupt changefulness, often associated with weakness of character or feebleness of mind; fickleness; a tendency to leap from whim to whim, with little indication of motive and practically no warning, (usually used derogatorily).

Captious (adj) – Being nitpicky; looking for faults in others, particularly of the minutest and least significant kind when grander faults are not readily apparent; being exacting or setting ridiculously high standards.

Compendious (adj) – Containing 'the scoop' on a large or important subject; The meat of the matter; including the abridged run-down of a topic.

Condescension (n) – The state of not looking down on someone; the act of speaking to others as equals, despite differences in rank or circumstances; the lowering of pride for the comfort of the company; in other words, the very opposite of how people usually use the word.

Conjecture (n) – A weakly supported assertion; a know-it-all's baseless effusions of opinion.

Consternation (n) – A state somewhere between slightly unsettled and a fit of hysterics, usually requiring a modifier or elaboration to pinpoint the degree of alarm; a panic attack prompted by some accident or incident; the perpetual state of a 'nervous Mary' or Patti panic'.

Controvert (v) – To provide an argument against; to suggest fallibility; to dispute the merits of or produce contradictory evidence against; to knock a mouthy know-it-all down a few notches.

Coquetry (n) – The art of seduction through the powers of flirtation; the siren call of feminine powers of persuasion; the intoxication and commandeering of masculine reason by the time-honored art of elegant flattery and the subtle baiting of physical allurements, such as batting eyes and swinging hips.

Countenance (n) - The look or expression of a person, in face, body language, or general air, particularly as it betrays thoughts, mood, or general character; sometimes it is more of an overall aura than any describable physical trait; this is a lost word that has no current replacement; with the decline of the word, so has declined the meaning and our understanding of it.

Coxcomb (n) – A cocky fool; one whose conceit has blinded him to reason; one whose self-absorption or delusions of grandeur has made him to look foolish.

Deference (n) – The act of deferring to the will or opinion of another; trust in another's decisions; unreserved trust; often the mindless and submissive yielding to someone greatly respected.

Deplorable (adj) – Downright awful; unpalatable; nauseating; something between giving you heartburn and sending you into a violent rage.

Deportment (n) – The behavior of a child, usually in front of or through the eyes of an adult; the mannerisms, posture, and general countenance of a student, a child, one one considered subordinate, in a formal setting, displaying demeanor and willingness to learn, and demonstrating the possessed degree of confidence and obedience.

Diffident (adj) – Timid; reluctant to push one's own will or acknowledge one's own worth, usually used for a person whose merits outweigh confidence.

Dissimulation (n) – The faking, hiding, or misrepresentation of something, often traits of character; affectation, particularly in the censure of negative traits of others which are possessed by the critic; hypocrisy.

Disultary (adj) – Supposed to be **Desultory**, meaning random, haphazard, without obvious direction; weakly navigated, without clear purpose; like the conversation of someone with an empty head who really wants to be talking.

Duplicity (n) – Deceitfulness; putting on a façade to fool someone; representing a person or situation to be different than reality, like one of those smooth talking, charming, silver-tongued snakes that woo the naïve.

Ebullition (n) – An eruption of thought or emotion; a tidal wave of opinions strongly felt; a swell in conversation.

Eclaircissement (n) - French word for clarification, particularly with the addition of information; a long version of a simple English word, used more for showing off than for eclaircissement.

Eclat (n) – French word for a big, showy to-do, or accomplishment, and if the French are calling it showy… think BIG.

Eleemosynary (adj) – Having to do with donations to charity or giving to the poor.

Enure (v) – To get used to or adjust to; to build up a tolerance for; to grow accustomed to or even come to appreciate something previously thought bad.

Epistolary (adj) – Having to do with written correspondence, generally of a personal nature; Involving the actual sitting and writing of a letter, not texting, not Skyping, or Facebooking, or Tweeting, or e-mailing, or any of the many other current modes of depressingly impersonal and grossly narcissistic self-dissemination of useless and utterly irrelevant personal information.

Evince (v) – To show or reveal an opinion, trait, or possession; to expose what is generally hidden or private.

Exculpate (v) – To make excuses; to clear one's name with evidence or explanation; to remove blame or doubt.

Expatiate (v) – To expand understanding through explanation or elaboration; to go on and on about a topic until the recipient can claim a far greater intimacy with the topic than either delicacy or desire would allow.

Expostulate (v) – To talk someone out of a certain action, course of behavior, or mode of thought; to scold or criticize.

Felicity (n) – A pleasant, peaceful sort of bliss; something between happy and elated, between the first bite of a warm pizza and quitting that job you hate.

Filial (adj) – Having to do with offspring, used to establish the child/parent association.

Forbearance (n) – Patience in overlooking the faults and behavior of another; tolerating any unpleasant circumstance; putting up with someone's bologna; biting your tongue when someone is doling out hot air.

Futurity (n) – That which belongs to, or is associated with, the future; the future consequences of the present.

Hauteur (n) – French word for haughtiness or arrogance... How do you not take that seriously?

Impertinence (n) – Presumptuousness; the assumption of a more intimate footing or higher station than reality should permit; an act of obnoxious intrusion; that guy jumping into water-cooler talk, in which he has never been welcome, giving advice to everyone on topics about which he knows nothing.

Importunity (n) - The state of obnoxiously nagging someone about something; the quality of annoyingly pressing someone on an issue (however justified), to the point of irritation or anger; the state of beating a dead horse.

Incredulity (n) – A state of disbelief or lending no credit to; often a state of hard-headed refusal to believe the obvious, even fooling one's self into disbelief.

Indefatigable (adj) – Going on and on without tiring; perpetuating ceaselessly; never 'calling it quits', often used negatively or sarcastically.

Indignation (n) – Disgust at something found offensive, usually some behavior or circumstance considered immoral, vulgar, or improper; that acid build-up in your stomach when someone's actions or attitudes grates so violently against your expectations and your sense of propriety and justice.

Indisposition (n) – The state of being ill or unwell, usually from slight physical ailment; the state of being hesitant or unwilling, in a state of refusal to comply with a request, demand, or expectation, often associated with hard-headedness or selfishness.

Inimical (adj) – Counteracting the effects of; standing in contradiction to; rendering moot or contrary to natural form.

Inimitable (adj) – One of a kind; unmatched or unsurpassed; literally unable to be imitated, usually denoting grandness or high quality.

Iniquitous (adj) – Just plain ole wrong; unjust; the sort of lip-curling offensiveness that makes you punch a wall and injure your hand.

Innoxious (adj) – Literally 'not noxious'; harmless; not irritating orcorrosive.

Intercourse (n) – Any exchange between individuals; two way communication; <u>not sex!</u>

Inure (v) – See **Enure**

Invective (n) – An insulting or censuring proclamation; a judgmental comment in the reproach of someone; a "burn" or "dis-ing" of someone.

Knocked Up (adj) – Exhausted; worn-out; brought to physical incapacity; <u>not "accidentally impregnated"</u>!

Lamentation (n) – Expression of sorrow or grief; a whining or 'bitching' session; a complaint, usually exaggerated and blown out of proportion, painting the speaker as the most wretched, misused creature to ever suffer human existence.

Languor (n) – Lack of exertion, or the ability to exert, due to fatigue, apathy, or any reducer of physical or spiritual energy; sloth; that 'Let the world burn around me, I'm not getting off the couch today' feeling.

Militate (v) – To have a profound, changing effect; to impact or alter severely.

Novitiate (n) - A novice; a rookie; one among those just breaking into a field of business; an upstart; a Johnny-come-lately.

Obsequiousness (n) – The state of yielding to another or humoring to impress or seduce; that 'Hey, you're right... you're always right' behavior, whether sarcastically used or in an authentic attempt to make someone feel good.

Obtrude (v) – To shove in the face of another person; to bombard another with your opinions, personality, or general presence, especially when not really wanted; to incite the silent response "Oh God, not him again" or "Just go away, damnit."

Obviate (v) – To nip in the bud; to render moot by anticipation; to put an end to something before it really begins.

Opprobrious (adj) – In a harshly scolding tone, given in response to shameful behavior; of or connected to disgraceful, embarrassing guilt.

Ostentatious (adj) – Having placed one's self on a pedestal for the viewing of others; conspicuously flaunting merits, real or invented; derogatory description of a loud show-off.

Panegyric (n) – A commendation or speech of praise, usually grand in style or presentation; this word is usually a compliment when the praise is given to another, but is used as an insult when one is praising one's self; it is the grandness that earns the word and therefore makes the self-praise all the more pathetic, as Jane Austen intends it.

Pecuniary (adj) – Having to do with money, debts, or payment.

Pensive (adj) - Thoughtfully depressed; stuck in a funk; coated with a sticky film of melancholy you just can't seem to scrape off.

Perspicuity (n) – The state of being plainly or clearly expressed, leaving no confusion; vividness, acuteness.

Pertinacity (n) – The state of being annoyingly persistent, resolute, or relentless in the pursuit of an action or opinion; the pressing and pressing and pressing an opinion or course of action, when all logic and reason stands in contradiction; the state of bugging the ever-living heck out of someone with a relentless pursuit of any kind, incurring the demand, "Would you just drop it already!"

Preponderate (v) – To out-do; to dictate the nature of; to force the general character of; to dominate; to tip the scales in favor of.

Profligacy (n) – The state of being way over the top, recklessly showy, or having 'piled it on thick'.

Prognostics (n) – Anticipatory thoughts of the future, often of a negative nature; pessimistic predictions; the proclamations of a Debbie-Downer.

Querulous (adj) – Whining, nagging, or complaining; in the state of pouring forth the hypochondriac's list of self-diagnosed ailments or misfortunes.

Recapitulation (n) – A brief review or summary, usually of something written or spoken; a brief clarification for the people who didn't get it the first time; a dumb-down of some communication for the good of those over whose head it soared unnoticed.

Remonstrance (n) – A harsh scolding or vehement objection to something considered wrong, offensive, or improper, sometimes designed to instruct, but often used to belittle, or make humble; to put someone in their place; to rub someone's nose in their own mistake.

Reprobate (v) – To censure; to harshly judge or condemn as wrong or inappropriate, generally from a loftier perch of rightness than whom or what is being condemned, used to represent a harsher degree than its synonyms.

Repartee (n) – Witty banter; a quip or sharp comeback in conversation; a conversation featuring wit and subtle cleverness; cocktail party talk among the academic elite.

Repine (v) – To whine; to complain in misery, usually to no purpose but in bringing down those around you.

Retrench (v) – To cut spending; to trim the fat; to squeeze within a reasonable budget, often with the re-evaluation of things previously considered necessities; altering a lifestyle to fit within the means.

Sanguine (adj) – Pleasantly optimistic; chipper; with a little spring in the step.

Sedulous (adj) – Not giving up; having stick-to-it-iveness; ardently and whole-heartedly seeing something to completion.

Solemnity (n) – The state of being serious or solemn, stuck in the mud, a buzz-kill, or just really, really into something.

Solicitude (n) – Concern or worry; a state of fear brought on by some evil or other; sometimes the actions one takes in response to the aforementioned state.

Succor (n) – Help given or a person who gives help; current vernacular has attached negative connotations associated with gullibility and has mistaken it with 'sucker', which of course is a lollypop, whose association with help or gullibility is thin at best.

Supercilious (adj) – Stuck-up in a hateful way; having assigned one's self to a lofty perch, deserved or not, then scorning all who dwell beneath that perch; much as people misuse 'condescending'.

Superfluity (n) – An abundance; a cup that run-eth over; a wasted excess, above what could possibly be used or needed.

Superlative (adj) – In the highest degree or of the highest order; surpassing all others; in such an extreme as to dwarf the company.

Taciturn (adj) – Tight-lipped; standoffish, either from shyness or contempt for the present company.

Tautology (n) – Redundancy; pointless reiteration or repetition of thoughts and words; when a person takes twenty minutes to describe something that took place in five.

Threadbare (adj) – Worn out; plain and simple; just like the same old beaten clichés or excuses you hear day in and day out.

Traduce (v) – To trash talk, talk smack, or scandalize the name of someone or something; to rip someone a 'new one'; to 'burn' someone.

Upbraid (v) – To blame or censure; to scold; to brow-beat with a harsh, judgmental lecture.

Vicissitudes (n) – Changes, usually occurring naturally, like the changes in appearances as one grows up or the development of a neighbourhood; alterations that occur through the normal passage of time.

Vitiate (v) – To corrupt or spoil; to twist into something distasteful; to ruin the purity of or render unappealing or not useful.

Volubility (n) – The use of many words; the state of being talkative; the relentless eruption of opinion, often with a sort of reckless, haphazard, and utterly disorganized flow, and often baring a negative tone or being negatively received.

Index of Phrases Spoken or Written by Primary Characters

Pride and Prejudice

Sense and Sensibility

Mansfield Park

Persuasion

Northanger Abbey

Emma

Lady Susan

References

[1] Austen, Jane. *Emma*. New York, NY: Scholastic
Book Services, 1967. Print.

[2] Austen, Jane. *Jane Austen's Letters*. Ed. Le Faye,
Deirdre. Oxford, U.K.: Oxford University Press,
1995. Print.

[3] Austen, Jane. *Lady Susan, The Watsons and Sanditon*.
New York, NY: Penguin Books, 2003. Print.

[4] Austen, Jane. *Love and Friendship and Other Early
Works*. New York, NY: Harmony Books, 1981.
Print.

[5] Austen, Jane. *Mansfield Park*. Ann Arbor, MI: Tally Hall
Press. 1997. Print.

[6] Austen, Jane. *Northanger Abbey*. New York, NY: Barnes &
Noble Classics, 2005. Print.

[7] Austen, Jane. *Persuasion*. New York, NY: The
Modern Library, 2001. Print.

[8]Austen, Jane. *Pride and Prejudice*. London, UK: Penguin Books, 1972. Print.

[9]Austen, Jane. *Sense and Sensibility*. New York, NY: Barnes & Noble Classics, 2004. Print.

[10]Austen, Jane and Bronte, Charlotte. *The Juvenilia of Jane Austen and Charlotte Bronte*. Ed. Beer, Francis. New York, NY: Penguin Books, 1986. Print.

CPSIA information can be obtained
at www.ICGtesting.com
Printed in the USA
JSHW062004241022
32076JS00001B/7